This book is a memoir. It reflects the author's present recollections of experiences over time. Some names and characteristics have been changed, some events have been compressed, and some dialogue has been recreated.

For June

A
Bittersweet
Goodnight

A MEMOIR OF LIFE,
LOVE AND FAMILY

Linda C Wright

Print ISBN: 978-1-54398-900-7

eBook ISBN: 978-1-54398-901-4

*If life is sweet, say thank you
and celebrate.
If life is bitter, say thank you and grow.*

CHAPTER ONE

I don't even know June's favorite color or what kind of books she liked to read or how she spent her time during the long empty days of retirement. June changed the diversity of her tastes like a chameleon, liking whatever food sat in front of her at the moment, or movie we selected to see, or blouse I wore. Whether we went to Outback or Applebee's, or sat on my back patio enjoying the fresh air, every meal we ate together turned out to be her most favorite. The colorful bouquet of lilies and roses I agonized over choosing for her birthday were always the most beautiful she'd ever seen and a Christmas gift of new stationery and postage stamps turned out to be exactly what she'd wished for.

But when life didn't agree with how June wanted it to be, she acted more like a mule, stubborn, impossible to reason with. Like the summer three of my father's grandchildren were being married, and no amount of convincing could get her to agree to attend even one of the weddings. My stepmother refused to go without my father, who by this time had been dead for ten years.

Or the time she didn't speak to my husband, Richard for several months after he commented on the price she paid to have some old, ugly wallpaper removed from the kitchen in her condo that had been on the walls when she moved in. He worked as an interior designer, knew the fair price of the job and probably could have called in a favor to have it taken down for free. When Richard told her she overpaid, she dug in her heels.

June always knew she was right and no one was going to tell her differently. She would never ask Richard or me for help of any kind, not with her finances, home repairs or ride to a good friend's funeral. She made her own arrangements. We gladly offered our assistance no matter what the problem because to us, June was family. To her we were something different. I'm not sure what separated us but I found through the many years I knew her that our relationship was like the brass ring on the carousel, coming closer, and floating farther away and always just slightly out of reach.

I don't even know the real color of her hair. After a certain age, all women keep that a secret but I knew June since I was eleven years old and I'm now sixty. Surely we spent time together before coloring the gray started. I began to color my own hair at forty, and when June moved across the street from us, she made her appointment for the same hairdresser I used, on the same day and time as me, every six weeks on a Saturday. I picked her up and together we went to the hairdresser. Our joke was we were getting all dolled up in order to pick up some cute guys at the grocery store where we headed for our weekly shopping trip right after our hair had been colored, cut and teased into perfection.

"June, I found an old picture of you. Your hair was blonde." I said. I didn't add 'while cleaning out your apartment' to the end of the sentence fearing it would trigger a temper tantrum. June wasn't happy since I turned her world upside down by moving her out of her familiar home to an unfamiliar assisted living unit.

She cocked her head to the left side trying to process my words.

"I never remember you as a blonde," I repeated.

"Oh, I think there was a blonde period at some point," she answered.

"You wore a beige knit suit. Who made those suits you sold like crazy back in the sixties?" I asked. "Butte Knits?"

June dreamed big for a woman of her day. As the first in her family to go off to college, she earned a teaching degree from Penn State and returned home to do what she was trained to do, teach. Small town life quickly lost its luster and somehow she managed to land a job at Kaufmann's, a department store in Pittsburgh. She moved to the big city to live with her aunt and uncle because a young woman of the times had only two choices. Live with family or rent a room at the YMCA. June started her career in ladies ready-to-wear and immediately found her calling.

"Kimberly Knits," she said.

"Ah. And you were holding Mia. I remember Mia in Seattle," I said.

Mia, June's miniature poodle, about fifteen pounds and black as night, came along when June married Dad.

"Molly," she corrected me.

Molly, a toy poodle, came after Mia. Again June chose a black dog, but Molly was much smaller than Mia. Molly weighed less than ten pounds but carried enough personality for a hundred. Her sister, Maggie, a gray version of Molly, who never turned away food of any kind and would snatch it from Molly's dish if given the opportunity, also came in a package deal. Maggie waddled like a duck while Molly ran circles around her.

Both dogs were kissers, licking my brother, Steve, and me during our summer visits to see Dad and June until we were covered with sticky dog slobber. The dogs made us giggle so we didn't really mind. It was more affection than we were shown by anyone else in our lives, none of who were great kissers or huggers, not even by dog standards.

"No, Mia. Don't you remember Mia?" I asked.

"No. Shana?"

A June who didn't remember her precious dogs was still hard for me to grasp. Her fading memory placed both of us on a rocky road searching for a new home where she could be watched over and cared for. It turned out to be a place neither of us wanted to be.

Dad and June bought Shana after Maggie and Molly got to old to live a comfortable life, from a person they referred to as a prominent standard poodle breeder after they moved to Tampa. Not that any of us cared where the dog came from as long as it gave us the hugs and slobbers we craved. June made sure her family and friends understood Shana came from a good pedigree.

It was June's way of letting the world know that she didn't let just anyone or anything into her home, only the best. That same mindset applied to her furniture, paintings on the walls and of course her clothing, showing off every chance she got. I learned over the years, in her mind she never made a mistake, even if I thought she had.

She picked out another black puppy from the litter and chose her name, however, Shana belonged to Dad. He drove her to the grocery store, allowing her to sit on the white leather seat of his Cadillac, took her for long walks and taught his dog with the fancy French haircut every stupid dog trick imaginable.

It's that vision of her beloved Paul with their very last pet that's the only image she's able to conjure up. The lineage of her favorite dogs is now tucked deep into the recesses of her mind. The thought of the two of them together is the only memory she can bring forward in this stage of her life.

"You were young in the picture. You had blonde hair. Remember?"

"No."

Dementia also acts as a chameleon, changing and adapting to the current situation. Answers to seemingly complex questions roll off June's tongue as if she was young and vibrant and knew everything that happened in the world today. If I asked who was the President, she'd most likely answer Obama, which was correct but if I asked her what she had for breakfast she could only tell me about her hot cup of coffee and nothing else, because she loved coffee and never started her day without it. I fell into the trap believing we were having an ordinary conversation as we'd done for years. Then she forgot her first and most precious dog.

June adored those dogs with every ounce of love in her heart. They were her children. She spoiled them rotten and cried for days when they became old and sick and had to be put to sleep. In my mind, it's a toss up whether the dogs or my father came first in her life.

When it was a dog's time to go, she made sure they no longer suffered. She gave them a peaceful ending to a rich and full life, a finale June longed to have for herself. I, too, wished for peace as June walked down the path to the end of her life, but I would struggle to help her find it.

"Goodnight June." I kissed her on the cheek. "I'll see you tomorrow."

"I love you," she answered.

"Love you too."

"We can only be said to be alive in those moments when our hearts are conscious of our treasures." – Thornton Wilder

CHAPTER TWO

My fingers fished for the envelope in the bottom of my overstuffed purse containing all the necessities of traveling. Hand sanitizer, antacids and cough drops were in the way of the one thing I needed at the moment. The key to June's apartment.

The yellowed, once white envelope with June's distinctive handwriting scribble of "Linda" in faded blue ink on the outside, which had been tucked away in my file cabinet for the past seven years, eluded my grasp this morning. Yesterday the key slid easily into the lock when I first arrived at June's condo. Today, the elusive piece of metal knew what awaited it and so did I. I dreaded the task of sorting, packing and cleaning all that lay ahead of me. Not being able to find the key only made my nerves bristle and my knees weak. After emptying half of the contents of my handbag onto the walkway floor, I finally unearthed the crinkled paper and pulled it out of the jumbled pile.

The deadbolt tightly gripped its place in the doorframe the way June had wanted it to for her protection from a threatening outside world. My shaking hands struggled to open the lock. Turning the key required Herculean strength and my attempts left deep, red creases on my thumb and fingers. I switched to my left hand, and it too lacked the muscle necessary to turn the key even a millimeter. With two-handed pressure, the lock finally released itself and I nudged the front door open with my shoulder. I'd look for some WD40 once I got inside.

The stench rushed up my nose knocking me back out onto the building's catwalk. A disgusting taste of stale smoke coated my mouth and a deep, restless cough rose in my throat and refused to stop. Here I stood, trying to believe June only smoked on the patio. She told me that story so many times I can still hear her voice in my head saying it. It's the first of many cover-ups I would discover over the next few weeks.

"I keep track of how many cigarettes I smoke each day." She pointed at a slip of paper she kept next to her seat on the sofa with dates followed by tick marks, the same number each day.

"Why do you keep track?" I asked.

"So I don't smoke too many and run out before I can get to the store." The logic made perfect sense for a woman in her nineties who never learned to drive a car and relied on other people to take her where she needed to go.

I retrieved a cough drop from my purse but it did little to douse the tickle in my throat. The stale odor of cigarettes locked up inside for two weeks during the Florida summer made itself at home inside of my sinus cavity and started my already aching temples pounding. The brief airing I attempted the day before had done little. The walls and draperies refused to relinquish all that belonged to June. They didn't want her to leave either. Someone new would paint the brown smoke tinged walls white again, throw the faded drapes in the trash and replace the carpet with stylish wood floors. Just like June, the old and worn furnishings would be forced into leaving their comfortable home.

My brief stop yesterday at the condo had been just that, brief. I didn't allow myself enough to time to be fully enveloped in the enormous task in front of me. I gave myself a week to get the apartment ready for sale. The added pressure I put on myself to raise the money for her care didn't allow me to be leisurely. Besides, I wanted to be at home, writing a funny story, taking a bike ride around the neighborhood or reading a captivating new book for the next meeting of my book club. The cavalry wasn't about to appear over the ridge. I was alone.

I poked around in the closet, choosing a few more items of clothing for June to wear. My sister, Susan, came from Ohio two weeks ago to pack June's suitcase for the move while I navigated June's doctor appointments, phone installation and furniture delivery from afar. I had my own busy agenda at home already arranged so Susan and I made a swap. She had the unpleasant task of extracting June from her apartment and depositing her at the Hawthorne Assisted Living before quickly returning to Ohio. I took the clean up duty.

Susan, however, left behind June's favorite white cardigan sweater. Yesterday she carried on how she needed it to throw over her shoulders to ward off the constant chill. I pulled it off the hanger along with a pair of black pants with pockets to stuff with the tissues June always carried with her, and an elastic waist to hold them up on her shrinking waistline. Susan packed every color of these once stylish old lady garments except the black. The color black was June's wardrobe staple and she didn't understand why they weren't hanging in her new closet.

I walked down the hallway into the living room and expected to see June sitting in her corner of the sofa, the place she always sat, the cushion now faded and showing an impression of June's skinny backside after many years of constant use. The other cushions were plump and full, a reflection into a solitary life.

I dumped my bag on the dining room table, something that never would be allowed if June still lived here. She kept it set with napkins and silverware, ready to serve a meal at any time. The table would become my workspace until my job here ended. The sooner I started the sooner I could get back home, kiss my husband, play with Ginger, my precious little sweet pea of a dog, and sleep in my own bed. Dreaming of those three simple things would make the 150 mile drive back home bearable, even bordering on pleasant no matter how much traffic I encountered on the road. At first glance those cozy comforts appeared to be a long way off.

Mostly however, I wished for the buzzing of the world around me to stop, for people who thought they knew better to abstain from forcing their views on how to care for an elderly woman on me. I prayed every hour on the hour, day and night, for all of this heartache to go away.

I looked around at June's life left behind. All her little knick knacks sat as they had for years, sprinkled across the coffee table, on the dining room buffet, and in full view on the antique candlestick table in the corner. A ten inch tall wooden carved French poodle, a dainty crystal slipper too small to even be Cinderella's and a long stemmed porcelain Cybis tulip the color of a ripe nectarine, all things I admired and came to love over the years, greeted me the same way they had for more than fifty years.

"Hi, Shana," I reached down to stroke the stationary poodle on its topknot.

A pack of pink Virginia Slims with a matchbook tucked under the cellophane wrapper remained on the end table next to her favorite spot on the sofa. Even her handwritten tally sheet and miniature yellow bridge pencil used to track her daily cigarette usage remained exactly as she left it, neatly aligned with the edge of the table.

I'm the chosen one to clean out the apartment and sell it to free up money for June's care. Susan, and her husband, Greg, and took on the task of getting a highly agitated and stubborn old woman out of here and into a new, fresh, clean apartment at the assisted living home. I can only imagine what that week was like for them. With my emotions on a dizzying rollercoaster ride, I'm exhausted just standing here and I wish I had a shoulder, anyone's shoulder to lean on. I'm not sure which one of us pulled the short straw in this lottery of life.

My other sister, Martha declined to help me at all with June. When asked, she announced she would support any decision I made, but would not be able to assist.

"You should just leave her alone," Martha told me. "Let her be."

Speechless, I couldn't find any words. Obviously Martha wasn't the step child getting phone calls at all hours of the day and night from people who were afraid she'd burn the condo down with her cigarettes and matches, who didn't want to be responsible if something happened to her, or who insisted she owed them money.

When given a choice, it's human nature to choose the path of least resistance, the easy way out. It takes courage to jump head first into the unknown. Courage is sadly lacking among my siblings it seems. I'm not putting myself on any pedestal, however, I wasn't given any choice. June assigned her power of attorney to me years ago, I was joint owner on her bank accounts, and the neighbors had my phone number. Therefore the easy way out was not an option for me.

I'm grateful for Susan's help during that week but standing in the middle of this mess, I'm annoyed by what she didn't do for June. Susan didn't know what June liked and disliked, what made her happy or sad. She left behind her favorite clothes. I'm the one who spent time with her, saw what she wore most often and the groceries she bought. I'm the only one who could do this job the way June wanted it done but I worried I didn't have the mental fortitude to accomplish it by myself. I knew many small details about her yet I felt I didn't know anything about how she lived her life.

"I told my kids, if anything happens to me, not to call my sisters. The two of you would have me moved out and the house sold in a blink of an eye," Martha rattled on.

"Then let's hope they have the smarts to find someone to take care of you when the time comes." I replied. "And I hope you aren't screaming at them a hundred times a day to leave you alone and go away."

Out of my frustration with my sister, came a rare twinkling of brilliance.

"June as you knew her is gone," Martha reminded me.

"I know. But when I talk to her on the phone, I want to believe she still knows who I am."

I needed Martha to tell me those very words at that very moment. I would, however, struggle to remember them. June didn't want to walk down this different path, and I didn't want to go with her. Change is the only certainty in life, and it's hard to accept especially when the end of the journey is going to be death.

I never bothered to ask my brother for help, nor did Susan, who lived nearby him in Ohio, saying it would be useless to ask. He'd never outgrown the emotionally unresponsive state we'd been raised in. I know in my heart he appreciates the unpleasant tasks his sisters have taken on for our stepmother, but it's not in him to participate. I'm OK with that.

Even though June never vocalized her feelings, she wanted only me to take care of her. Although my siblings maintained a relationship with her over the years, calling at the holidays, sending photos of their families and occasionally making a visit to see her, it was me she spent the most time with. I lived nearby until only recently and took her out to eat on every birthday, learned how to fix her vodka just the way she liked it, and years ago drove her back and forth to the hospital to see her beloved Paul when he was sick. June thought I had the experience to make decisions the way she wanted them.

In the middle of June's once neat and orderly life, I stood playing God. She wasn't dead, only walking down a road that could be short or long, only time would tell. Years ago, without telling me, she assigned me the job of dividing up her memories and sending them off into the great unknown. The recipients however, may never hear the charming and romantic tales of my father bringing home a complete set of Waterford wine glasses as a surprise for his wife's birthday or the three miniature Lenox swans trimmed in gold he had wrapped in separate boxes to give to her for Valentine's Day, the day of love.

Maybe they would take one look and say "What the hell is this?" before tossing it in the trash or hauling it off to the Goodwill. What June wanted was what I was going to do my best to give her. The warmth of my tears trickled down my cheeks and I quickly rubbed them away. Wasting time crying would not get this smelly apartment cleaned out any faster and move June and me onto the next phase of our lives.

"Everything is going to be alright.
Maybe not today, but eventually."
— Anonymous

CHAPTER THREE

On a gloomy and gray Sunday afternoon in May, my brother, Steve and I settled in to watch television in the basement of our large suburban home in Cleveland. In 1967 we had only three channels to choose from and if we manipulated the rabbit ears just right, we might be able to get the roller derby on UHF. Otherwise we were stuck watching Bishop Sheen. Mom dragged us to church that morning so we didn't feel we needed any more saving. Today we lucked out. *The Three Stooges* came on.

These were also the days before TV remote controls. Since I was only eleven and Steve, thirteen, he ordered me to change the stations while he stretched out on the sofa and barked out the instructions.

The door at the top of the stairs creaked open. My mother's heavy foot landed on the steps.

"Quick!" Steve whispered. "Change the channel. Hurry."

You see, we weren't allowed to watch the Three Stooges. My mother declared them too violent and off limits. I was young and fast and we rarely got caught. If we did, it would result in no television for the rest of the day. Boring! So we avoided punishment at all costs. Tarzan and Jane were swinging through the jungle by the time Mom reached the bottom step.

"I need to talk to you," she said. "Turn off the TV."

I obeyed, cutting off Tarzan's jungle cry midstream.

She sat down in a chair facing us and took in a deep breath. At that moment, clouds covered the tiny bit of sunshine available that day, changing the light coming through the large windows in the walkout basement from dull to dark.

Mom let out her breath. "Your father has married again. I was hoping I could get him back but I can't."

My mother stared at us, I think, looking for some kind of reaction. Neither my brother nor I were the reactive types. From our point of view, nothing about our lives had changed since our parent's divorce. We still lived in our large sprawling home, went to the same school, played with the same friends and my father wasn't home. That was no different from when my parents were married.

Dad worked as a merchandise manager for the May Company, a department store chain in Cleveland. He traveled a lot, and worked late on Mondays and Thursdays. Between Thanksgiving and Christmas we never saw him unless my mother dressed us up, packed us in the car and drove us to the Rapid Transit for a trip downtown to his office. We got paraded around and all the ladies who worked for him would ooh and ahh over us. In fact June probably led the charge in order to impress my father on at least some of those occasions. We had no idea who she was or any recollection of meeting her. My mother was most likely clueless about June too, but smart enough to know this was the only way her children would spend any time with their father. The meaning of the term Black Friday had been drilled into our tiny child brains from a very early age. It's what kept us clothed, fed and housed in a very nice manner.

Dad changed jobs a lot too. In my eleven years of life I lived in Pittsburgh, Detroit, Minneapolis and now Cleveland. When we arrived here in January 1961, I was enrolled in Mrs. Deming's first grade class. They had only made it to the letter "M" in the alphabet, but knew how to count by 5. In my old school, I had completed the entire alphabet but hadn't made it much past two plus two in the math department. Steve had to get some tutoring he was so far behind his third grade class in math.

As a little girl, I was very shy so being thrust into a new school frightened me. I never made friends easily and here the other kids made fun of me when they found out I couldn't add. At an early age I learned not to get myself too attached to anything especially people, fearing they'd tease me. With a moving truck waiting around the corner, I knew any friends I did make would soon be yanked away from me with no hope of ever returning. That my parents were no more as a couple was not as earth shattering to us as children as I'm sure it was to Mom.

"Her name is June. They met at the store," she said. "Your father has started a new job in Seattle and June will be moving there soon. I'm hoping you can get to meet her before she leaves."

At that moment Mom's life had already changed dramatically. She had to sell a house, find a new one for us to live in and look for a job. She never worked outside the home but she had four children to take care of with probably only some court decided child support to rely on.

Our lives hadn't changed yet, at least not that we took the time to worry about. As children, we weren't aware of the full impact of my parents' divorce and the addition of a new stepmother into our fractured family circle. We had no idea of what kind of real change was yet to come into our lives. Changing the channel on the television was about as far into the future as we could see.

Neither Steve nor I responded. We only did what was normal for us. Nothing. Mom got up from her chair and trudged back up the stairs. Once we heard the basement door close, we turned the Three Stooges back on just as Moe tweaked Curly's nose.

"It is only those who never do anything,
who never make mistakes." – A. Favre

CHAPTER FOUR

Rummaging through the pile of notes on the dining room table, I pulled out a list I received from the lawyer. When I called him for some advice after the incident, what I got was this inventory June painstakingly wrote on a yellow legal pad several years ago and added to her will. He mailed the amendment to me along with a bill for his time. I added lawyers to the succession of people wanting money from me. He can get in line behind the rest who now think I'm an easy target to get to June's money.

Only a month ago did June finally agreed to allow me to become joint owner on her bank accounts.

"Just in case," I told her.

She wouldn't go to the bank with me to sign the papers, so I went alone. I showed the bank employee the power of attorney document and asked to be added to her checking account. He typed on his keyboard then stared at his screen for a few minutes before announcing June was an old woman and I needed to be added to all of her accounts. I didn't argue even though I didn't really think it was necessary at the time. She had one hundred and fifty thousand dollars in the bank and now it was my job to make that last, however long that might be.

Slowly unfolding it, I read the lawyer's paper for the first time.

Stephen

Wedgewood china pieces, Lenox swans and small vase

Susan

Toby and Hummel mugs and figurines

Martha

Diamond engagement ring with white gold band

Linda

Miscellaneous Wright family papers, pictures, albums.

I stopped reading. The paper fell from my hands while my thoughts ran like thoroughbreds in the Kentucky Derby being feverishly whipped by their jockeys to go faster and faster. Except with each stride the finish line moved further and further out of sight. I'm the one sitting in this hot, stinky apartment in charge of disposing of an old woman's possessions and all the pretty trinkets I adored being surrounded with every time I came to visit, are now the property of someone else. Maybe I didn't say often enough how much I'd grown to admire her things. Maybe she never listened. Maybe she had a bigger plan for me.

"Why does Susan get the Hummels?" I said out loud. "She'll never think to dust them off once she puts them on a shelf. And Martha doesn't wear any jewelry. What's she going to do with June's diamond ring?"

I'm the one who knew all the stories of how she came to own most of these things. June loved to tell them. Every time she did, I said,

"My father went to the store and actually picked out the Lenox swans for you?"

June smiled, "He did. And he had them gift wrapped each in a separate box."

For many years, the mother and her cygnets were perfectly positioned to appear to be swimming across a shimmering pond on the glass topped coffee table. The thought of my brother adoring the flock of elegant, gold trimmed porcelain birds became more than my cluttered mind could fathom.

What woman wouldn't want to be given diamonds, regardless of whom they came from? The jewelry I often admired because it was handsome and tasteful, not because I wanted to wear it, too old ladyish for me, would now be worn on someone else's hands. I wouldn't get the chance to reset any of it into a piece that would remind me of June and our good times together. Even worse, the rings and bracelets would be tucked away never to see the light of day, and most likely sold at the pawnshop for pennies on the dollar. The gifts Dad had chosen for his wife were being tossed out into the universe, never to be seen or heard from again. I would never see, hold or admire any of these precious keepsakes ever again.

None of these were feelings I was used to having. I never had a temper, preferring instead to keep my emotions inside, like I was trained to do as a child. I wanted to think I let go of at least some of what I had tucked away when June and I had our frequent gossip sessions with my glass of white wine and hers of vodka and a splash of water. The secrets about my life I divulged to her meant nothing. Maybe I let her order too many of the half price happy hour drinks and once drunk and she forgot everything I said minutes after I said it. I think she wanted to tell me something she never got around to saying.

During those meals we never talked about how much our lives intertwined, what we meant to each other. We never spoke of the keepsakes adorning our homes silently admired before each home cooked meal served at well-used dining room tables over the years. Trashy gossip about neighbors and coworkers fueled our conversations. Friendship, love and family never entered in. If we had spoken of these things, I might not be so surprised at this moment at the loss of her material possessions, things I thought I held dear.

The bigger point however, June still lived. Assisted living care was expensive and I took a big leap when I selected her new home. I'd be spending down what was left of her money at a lightening fast clip just to pay the monthly rent. I wanted to be certain she'd be well taken care, and that comes at a steep price. Would I have to move her again when she ran out of funds and went on Medicaid? It all depended on how long she would live. The mere thought made me break out in a sweat. The palm of my hands became clammy, leaving their damp, sticky imprint on the infamous list.

My own mother dwindled down her meager savings and after a year or so in a nursing home she was forced onto Medicaid. That left her a prepaid funeral plan and approximately three thousand dollars to her name. Kidney failure, osteoporosis and dementia made her helpless, spending the last five years of her life in a New York City skilled care facility before she succumbed to blood poisoning one week after her eightieth birthday.

Mom had more health issues, less money and was much younger than June when she faced long term nursing care. She also went kicking and screaming to a place she didn't want to be. Martha and her husband, Tom navigated Medicaid with the nursing home via long distance from Michigan. Every couple of months, I joined Martha in New York City to check on Mom but after awhile she didn't know who we were when we came to visit.

Mom had a boyfriend, also named Paul, like my father, who worked as a doorman at a fancy apartment building in the city. He was much younger, more like the age of her children, and didn't want to know us. We knew he came to see her regularly because the nurses rolled their eyes when we asked about him. As long as he kept Mom entertained, we didn't have to. She'd rather have been with Paul than any of her children even before she stopped recognizing our faces. None of us had a close or loving relationship with her, or she with us. If this Paul made her happy, that was the best thing we could ask for.

"I know!" I said aloud after a flash of brilliance lit up my brain. "I won't tell anyone about the list and I'll sell it all on EBay." A plausible idea since the lawyer knew how to contact only me in June's case.

I used to be familiar with the markings for Hummels and Royal Doulton Toby mugs when I sold them while working in Gimbels Pittsburgh china and gifts department, my first job out of college. Long ago, however, I filed that mundane information away. Millenials didn't bother drinking their wine out of fancy cut crystal glasses or polish sterling silver flatware so the market for these things would probably be pretty small. The energy needed to do an extensive Internet search on the value of June's collectibles drained me at the moment. So how much money could all this stuff generate? Probably not enough to cover the fee for a box of Depends for more than a couple of months.

A salty tear landed on my lip. Reading the list again, I prayed the water in my eyes had clouded the words on the page. I wanted desperately for it to say something else. Something that wouldn't bring tears to my eyes and put a lump in my throat.

I read it again. The words on the page hadn't changed. This time my tears splattered with a plop on the damp sheet of paper. I wanted badly to give up the idea of trying to hold on to what didn't belong to me and move on to my next task.

*"We don't meet people by accident.
They are meant to cross our path for
a reason."*

CHAPTER FIVE

Soon after that day in the basement when my mother announced my father had remarried, our large house in the suburbs went up for sale. With Susan and Martha off at college and determined to keep my brother and me in the same school district, Mom rented a spacious apartment in a brand new complex on busy Chagrin Boulevard about three miles away. Downstairs it had a living room, dining room and kitchen, and upstairs three bedrooms and a bath. The dining room had a large picture window overlooking the parking lot.

That first summer Steve and I figured out how to keep tabs on the coming and goings of everyone important who lived in the new neighborhood which turned out to be an exciting change from our usual traipsing through the woods and wading in the creek behind the old house. If there was news to be spread, we knew it first. From the rich divorcee who lived across the hall with her poufy hair and bright orange lipstick with a parade of boyfriends through her door, to the slick, leather clad greaser kids who picked a fight with anyone who looked at them cross-eyed. Steve and I could have written the neighborhood gossip column.

In order to break the news gently to us once more, this time Mom sat us down on the sofa in the living room. Without a basement, the Three Stooges were a thing of the past. The one and only television resided in the living room. We had no escape.

"I believe you children need to get to know June. I've invited her over for dinner on Saturday night." Her voice quivered but she remained firm with her words.

We stared blankly at her, our usual response to Mom's announcements.

"I'm picking her up at the Rapid Transit at 5:30 and bringing her back here for dinner," Mom told us.

Susan and Martha, both home from college for the summer, already knew about the dinner party. It was a familiar pattern in our household, the separation of the two college girls and the two younger innocents. My sisters knew everything before I did. Steve didn't care; being the only boy he was oblivious to the politics of the women in the family. Even at eleven years old, I knew I didn't want to be left behind. I hated being the last to know everything.

Although I was only two years younger than Steve, I was eight years younger than Susan, the oldest. It's a big gap when you're in elementary school and your older sisters are in high school and headed to college. They had boyfriends. I still hated boys. They watched soap operas while I watched cartoons of Rocky and Bullwinkle. My sisters wore garter belts with nylon hose and hung their bras to dry in the bathroom. I wore white lacy anklets with black patent leather Mary Janes.

It wasn't until I was in college myself that Mom announced to me one day that I was an accident. With two girls and a boy already, the family was complete until I appeared. An oops, she called it. Mom, in her misguided effort to show love to her children, only distanced me more. Long before this announcement I'd been searching for the parental love and sibling connections that eluded me. This helped to explain why I felt left behind in the family dynamics.

Mom gave us all strict instructions before she left, set the table, brush your teeth and put on a clean shirt. She and June would be back in a half an hour. My mother had never been much of a housekeeper. Straightening up the tiny living room and vacuuming the little bit of carpet took all of what little energy she had left. Inviting June had been her idea after all, and I'm sure the drive to the Rapid Transit was the longest ride of her life.

To this day I wondered why June agreed to come. I never figured out why Mom wanted to put herself in that position. She cared about us in a way that she didn't want her children to be afraid or feel uncomfortable around June. I understand that. Why my mother was the one to introduce us to our new stepmother and not my father is a mystery. June told me once, Dad didn't want her to come to dinner that night but she thought it was the right thing to do.

Steve and I took our usual places at the window. We waited. And watched.

Our white Ford sedan came around the corner and pulled into our assigned parking spot right underneath our lookout.

"They're here," I shouted.

A small, petite woman opened the door on the passenger side closest to us and stepped out of the car. Her hair had been rolled, set and teased in a beauty parlor fashion. She wore a dark blue sheath dress with a string of white pearls. Clutching a small leather bag and wearing matching sling back pumps, her heels clicked on the sidewalk. She looked like she stepped right out of Vogue Magazine. Our own mother never dressed so stylishly.

Mom looked fat and dowdy by comparison. My mother didn't just look fat she was fat, as round as she was tall. As kids, her obesity was a constant source of embarrassment for us. All my friends had skinny moms. Seeing the discarded wife and the new wife side by side made my father's choice all the more clear to me. As much as I wanted to believe love isn't shallow and belongs in the heart, outward appearances are what first catches a person's eye. Mom appeared old and worn out next to the fashionable and slender, June.

Susan turned down music blaring from the small gray plastic radio we kept on the bookshelf, left on all day long as a way to squelch the silence that allowed our thoughts to dwell in how suddenly the boundaries of our lives had shrunk. The music of the sixties allowed my college aged sisters to dream of finding love and escaping our broken family. For me, blowing off some steam dancing the twist or the swim or the mashed potato helped me to forget I could no longer ride my bike down the big hill on Kersdale Road or scour the woods behind our house looking for wildflowers. My world had gotten significantly smaller.

June stood in the doorway, while my mother did the introductions, oldest to youngest.

"This is Susan and Martha. And Steve and Linda."

I lowered my chin to my chest, not sure if I wanted to make eye contact with her.

"It's nice to meet all of you. I'm glad Sallie invited me tonight," June said.

I don't remember what we talked about or what we had for dinner that night. I do know the conversation never waned. It was still light out when Mom drove June back to the Rapid Transit, so she didn't stay long and drag out what was most likely an exhausting night for her and my mother both.

When I married Richard at age thirty-one and he was forty-four, I became a stepmother to a twenty year old, Pam. I never mothered her, she had one of her own and she was an adult. I only offered advice as best as I could and when it was asked for. One of the first lessons of marriage I learned was to never come between a father and his daughter. The daughter always wins. Never having been the jealous type, to this day I have a very friendly relationship with Joan, Richard's first wife. I didn't know it at the time, but I absorbed the nuances of stepmotherhood and the proper treatment of ex-wives around the dinner table that night.

"Can you believe she came to meet us?" I asked my sisters after they left.

Even in my pre-teen mind, I understood my father didn't like my mother any more and June was the other woman that had seduced him into marriage. Dinner had been pleasant enough but I still wasn't sure what to think about her. She wasn't what I would call pretty. She had a wide nose with big nostrils, thin lips covered in thick red lipstick and poufy golden hair. Mom wasn't pretty either, and she never learned how to style her own hair or apply makeup tastefully to enhance what little she had. It must have been a thin figure versus a chubby one, makeup versus none and teased hair versus no hairdo that attracted my father. I couldn't see any other differences between them.

"No. I can't," Susan answered with the usual firm tone in her voice.

"What are we supposed to call her?" I asked.

Stepmother sounded so cruel and Cinderella-ish. June didn't seem mean or demanding to me, but what was she? Was she my parent? No, I had two of those and neither had stopped their parenting ways as limited and inconsistent as it was. Was she my friend? No, Georgia was my friend at school. I couldn't conceive of the notion that anyone over the age of twelve would be my friend.

"I don't know. She never said," Susan answered. "Let's just try 'June' and if she doesn't like it, too bad."

My parents had taught us to respect adults. I didn't call any of my friends' parents by their first names, only Mr. Mitchell or Mrs. Adams. Calling my stepmother June went against everything I ever learned. If my older sister said to call her by her first name, then that's what I would do but I feared it would get me into trouble. So there June remained, in some kind of childhood limbo, not mother, not friend, not wicked step mother. And there she would stay, at least for the time being.

*"Even if you are on the right track,
you'll get run over if you just sit there."
— Will Rogers*

CHAPTER SIX

I crumpled the paper in my fist and tossed it across the room. The past few months had been rough since June turned ninety-one and I wanted to believe the hard part was over now she was safely settled in her room at the assisted living home. My reaction to the amendment to her will however, told me that wasn't to be. After Dad died, June lived on her own until well into her nineties, a fact I should be grateful for. Overall she lived a happy and healthy life until all hell broke loose and I ended up sitting smack dab in the middle of the fire.

A long list of circumstances led me here but for my sisters, one they didn't have any knowledge of. I couldn't shake it out of my head. Our frame of reference would always be different, me on one side and everyone else on the other with June trapped in the middle. The memory that divided us played out like a movie.

Two days before June's ninety-first birthday, I receive a frantic call from Susan while out riding my bicycle around the neighborhood. I learned to carry my phone with me for times like this. Calls came in at all hours, always jostling my mind and setting me on edge not knowing who was on the other end wanting some kind of help I had no idea how to give.

"Edible Arrangements tried to make a delivery to June and she told them to go away. She wouldn't let them in," Susan said, her voice loud, her words quivering.

My hunt for answers on the best way to care for June was going nowhere. I spent each morning making calls to home care services and senior service organizations. Each call yielded more confusion. I called June every day and she seemed to be stable during our conversations. I realize now however, the dementia lizard fooled me once again.

"Let me call 911. I'll call you back later and let you know what I find out," I said.

What I didn't tell my sisters and brother was June had threatened to kill herself a few weeks before. I made the two and half hour drive to see her, made sure she knew when I would arrive and her plan was for me to find her dead. Only I knocked on her door before she tied the plastic bag over her head. I didn't want to explain and listen to any of them gush over how horrible that must have been for me. I know it and it hurt me. They wouldn't have been able to do anything to help, nor would they offer.

None of them can possibly understand how I feel. Why June chose to put me through that continues to gnaw at my being. I'm a coward, leaving her alone, running out on her. I should have gotten help right then and there but instead I walked out. Here she is pulling the same stunt again; only Susan thinks June is singling out Susan and her birthday gift.

"I spoke to Rosemary and she already called the paramedics," Susan said.

"Pray Susan, they find something wrong with her and take her to the hospital. It's the only hope to get her out of that place," I said.

I called the Delray Beach Police Department and was told the paramedics had been dispatched to June's apartment. The operator took down my number and would have them contact me.

I waited. After what seemed like hours, the phone rang.

"Hello, this is Brian Miller from Delray Beach Fire Rescue. We're here with June."

"Is she OK?" I asked.

"We can't take her to the hospital. Her vital signs are normal," he said.

My lungs suddenly emptied themselves of all air. "Is there any way you can get her out of there? She's so darn hard headed," I asked.

"Unfortunately, no. But I don't think she should be living alone." He began to laugh. "She just lit up a cigarette."

I chuckled too. "That's June."

"The air conditioning is working fine. She had it turned off. It was about 90 degrees in here but it's starting to cool down," he said.

I immediately knew what June was up to. She turned off the air-conditioning on purpose. Not wanting to celebrate another birthday she thought up another hair brained idea, this time to cook herself to death. Ashamed of myself for not doing anything the first time she threatened suicide, again I believed June when she promised to cooperate with me. My guilt in what my sister and June's neighbors might think of me crowded out my ability to properly care for her.

The paramedic handed the phone to Rosemary. She's crazy with worry, then to Darlene, another neighbor who lived down the hall, who demanded I do something about her now.

I replied using what's become my standard line.

"Darlene, I appreciate all you and Joe did for her over the years. I'm working with an agency to send in an aide to help her. It's been difficult to find someone because of her smoking." I exhaled. "Please know I'm trying my best and someone will be with her in the next couple of days."

I told a little white lie. All the home care agencies I'd contacted over the past few weeks refused to work at the frantic pace I felt necessary. I had no clue when I could get someone to assist with June's care. I had five more agencies on my list to call.

"I'm not going to be responsible if anything happens to her," she replied.

"No one is asking you to be, Darlene. Thank you for all your help," I answered.

Next the paramedic gave the phone to June.

"Linda. Why is everyone making such a fuss? I hate it," she whined.

"Leave the air conditioning on. It's hot outside in the summer," I said knowing she paid no attention to my instructions.

"OK. I'll do what you tell me. Just let me stay home," her voice hitched.

"Behave yourself, June and then you can stay put." I spoke as if she were ten years old.

"I'll be good. I promise," she said.

June had to convince Rosemary and Darlene, not me. There wasn't a snowball's chance in hell I was going to believe any such a promise ever again. That's the promise I made to myself after I hung up the phone.

June's stubbornness had always been one of her most prominent traits. These days she dug her heels in even deeper than I'd ever seen her do in the past. The mind trying to overcompensate for what the body could no longer control started the battle neither could win. I struggled with knowing when she knew what was going on and when she didn't. I believed she knew precisely the reactions her deliberately planned yet skewed actions could elicit from me, which was an integral part of her overall strategy. She'd been the one in control all her life and even though her mind was failing, the muscle memory of being in charge remained fully in place.

In the deep recesses of my mind, June was still the same June I talked and laughed with over a drink. When she assured me she ate dinner last night, I believed her. Why wouldn't I? God played a cruel trick on all of us. I trusted her but deep down in the dark trenches of her mind she knew I was the one she had to deceive in order to get what she wanted. That's how dementia works only I couldn't find any information about this cruel subtlety spelled out in any Google search. So I too, remained in the dark.

I never abandoned my moral code since respecting my elders was ingrained in my being from an early age. Knowing little about how to deal with an elderly person with dementia, I didn't know I needed to find a new way to communicate with her. The usual "Hi June, how are you doing?" would no longer generate a truthful answer.

* * *

My self imposed pity party over, I gathered up a pile of newspapers on the floor, grabbed the full garbage bag and headed down the hall to the trash chute. One job done, one hundred thousand more to go. I packed up the unused Life Alert necklace and alarm box and set it outside the front door for pickup. Mentally exhausted already, I wrestled with my choices for the next task. I wanted to choose one I could do without crying or feeling weak at the knees.

I'd better get busy and find the box of family papers. It's the only thing on this list I don't know where or what it is and it was the only thing I would take home. None of June's pretty things belonged to me now even though I needed only one fancy knickknack to remember her by. I dreaded how I might react when I found the box, and I feared I might find some deep dark secret inside. If June could no longer speak truthfully to me, had she been lying to me about something else over the years and I'd been totally unaware? I wondered.

June paid her bills at a small desk under the window in the spare bedroom. Unlike my father, who'd been know to write out a check for the electric bill within minutes of opening the mailbox, June organized her bills in date order in a letter rack. A book of stamps was kept handy in the corner of the drawer, and two pens were stored in a cracked coffee mug on the windowsill.

I chose to see what useful information the desk might hold, and was instantly sorry I had. As if a tornado had landed in the tiny workspace, papers lay every which way like they'd been dumped out of a garbage can instead of being placed in the wastebasket and taken down the hall to the incinerator. The wood top of the desk wasn't visible, nor was the checkbook or the mug of pens. I slowly backed myself out of the room returning to the relative safety of the living room.

So much for choosing something that wouldn't make me cry. Initially I involved myself in her life because Dad wanted me to, but today I was here with compassion and loyalty. I wanted to be someone June could count on too. I retrieved the crumpled list I'd thrown in the corner and read the remainder of the names on it.

Surrounded by her life, a life we shared in so many ways for so many years, she wanted me to pack it all up and send it off. Of course I knew my two sisters and my brother, but I never met anyone else whose name she wrote on the list except for her goddaughter, Kathy.

June had one sister, Marion, who passed away in her sixties of pancreatic cancer. She died shortly before my Valentine's Day wedding in 1987 and in typical blushing bride fashion; I panicked a little, wondering if my father would get back from the funeral in time to walk me down the aisle. He insisted on driving from Florida to Pennsylvania in January, snow or no snow.

Robin, Larry, Jim and Peter were Marion's children. While I knew their names, I never met them. The list clearly stated what belonged to them, including her father's telegraph machine he used while working for the railroad and the miniature wooden shoes he brought back from Europe after his service in World War I.

I never knew why, but for some reason the two sets of children were never invited to mix. Not a drop of June's blood flows through my veins yet I'm the chosen one. The blood relatives are nowhere to be found in her time of need. I turned off her phone when I turned the new one on at the assisted living. The number changed. June insisted she spoke to all of them often. Let's see how long it takes for one of them to contact me when they hear the disconnection message from the phone company.

Kathy was June's goddaughter. I never understood the concept of godparents, but she always referred to Kathy as that. Being raised Presbyterian I don't have godparents. When a baby is baptized, the entire congregation pledges to take care of the child. Kathy's mother, Nan was June's best friend since childhood. I assumed June stood up in church and officially received the title of godmother, but it's hard to picture. I never knew June to go to church or to show any kind of interest in a higher power.

Nan was a creative woman, something June wasn't; who hand-made my Christmas cards for me for years. I placed my order with Nan every July and excitedly opened the box of cards when it arrived in November. My friends loved receiving the fat jolly Santa with the wispy white cotton beard, and Rudolph with a red felt nose. The card I loved the most was the year she crafted the angel who seemed to float on air while attached to a glittery white card. With much sadness I was forced to purchase store bought cards, after Nan lost her life to breast cancer. It's now a struggle to find the right greeting after having sent Nan's glittering handiwork for years to all my friends and family.

Nan and Kathy came to visit June once after Dad died. June cooked her Pennsylvania Dutch pot roast and Nan showed me her newly created line of thank you notes with dried flowers prettily arranged on the front. We had so many laughs that night it was as if I had known them all my life. In a way I had, through June. She adored them both and spoke of them often but again kept her most precious friends from me for all these years. I don't know why.

Once again the knife at the bottom of my gut began stabbing at my insides. I opened the sliding glass door, walked over the ramp some handyman had fashioned for her so she wouldn't trip over the door tracks, and sucked in a breath of hot, humid but fresh air. I wiped a puddle of green water from the seat of one of the white plastic chairs gracing the tiny, screened patio. I dried the seat with a thin and worn hand towel that had been left draped over the back of a chair to be available for this very purpose. A matching plastic table wedged itself between them.

On the table, I found June's ashtray still full of cigarette butts. Were these lipstick ringed stubs June's final smoking frenzy before my sister marched her out the door, put her in the car and drove her to the Hawthorne Residence? Her makeup went on first thing every morning but did she take extra care that day knowing she'd be meeting many new people? Did she throw her tracking list to the wind during that final hour? Was she leisurely having her morning smoke unaware she'd wake up tomorrow in a strange bed without her cigarettes on her nightstand? I wanted to believe it was the latter, enjoying her final smoke.

I knew the ashtray well. It came with June to every home she shared with Dad. White porcelain, in the shape of a seashell, trimmed in gold. More than likely the piece was a gift from a ladies dress manufacturer trying to win her business as a buyer for a major department store. Etched across one side, her name, 'June D. Coackley'.

I'm not sure when I learned her given first name was not June. Her given name had been Dorothy June Cockley. She hated the name Dorothy and at some point in her life told people to call her June. I had only ever known her as June.

The odd thing was she never legally changed her name. When I started handling her affairs, all of her accounts were titled as June D. Wright. Social security and the long-term care insurance company never questioned me about a difference in her legal name. My guess was when she went to social security back in 1967 to change her name to Wright, she told them to switch the Dorothy and the June while they were at it. In the days before computers, those things were possible.

However, her last name, since my siblings and I were never introduced to her family, remains a mystery to me. I vaguely remember her telling me one time she added the 'a' because she tired of people pronouncing it "Cockley" with a short 'o' as in slang for a male body part. She wanted it pronounced with a long 'o' as in a popular, soft drink. Once she took my father's name, her maiden name fell off the radar, but the golden spelling of Coackley remained on the ashtray.

Through the years I'd known her, June often put on airs that she was someone better or different than herself like switching her first and middle names, or changing her last name by adding a letter and hoping no one else would notice. She loved to casually referred to the man down the hall who she paid to drive her to her doctor appointments as her "driver" in order to impress her neighbors and make sure they knew she was self sufficient and had money. I didn't understand why she couldn't just be June. All the time we'd spent together had I been gossiping and laughing with June or someone she imagined herself to be in her mind?

Sitting next to a pile of cigarette butts did little to clear my scratchy throat or ease the pounding in my head behind my eyes. I didn't stay on the patio for long and took the ashtray with me when I went back inside. I dumped the whole thing, gold trimmed shell, stale butts and her made up name into the trashcan.

The green eyes of jealousy glared at me from around the room. Did I feel I was the only one entitled to her precious things since I'm the one who knew her best? Am I angry I'm the only one here; angry I can't leave here until this job is done, or angry June can't live on her own any longer? By poking through all of her cherished possessions, things that were always in the same spot no matter which home she lived in, something about them now seemed jumbled, haphazard. I couldn't make sense of how she decided who got which piece. Maybe nothing about June made any sense to me anymore. Her constant changing to fit into situations or impress different people was her disguise and I never really knew this woman, my stepmother, my friend, and a member of my family. A person I had known for more than fifty years.

I picked up the crinkled, yellow list and tried to flatten it out. Writing Kathy's name on a pink post it note, I placed it on the small gold and cut crystal umbrella that resided on the sofa's end table. I wrote more names on the sticky note pad and walked around the room placing them on June's precious items I would never see again.

"Not all those who wander are lost."
— J.R.R. Tolkien

CHAPTER SEVEN

That summer Steve and I were packed up and shipped off to spend our allotted three weeks per the divorce decree with Dad and June in Seattle. We flew all by ourselves so someone thought we were sensible and grown up enough to make the six-hour flight across the country alone.

We weren't strangers to flying. Mom used to joke I'd been flying since before I was born. Those were the days when the stewardess passed out chewing gum to keep your ears from popping as the plane took off. I remember once our family flew from Minneapolis to Detroit to spend Christmas with my grandparents. When the stewardess held a black tray filled with brightly colored pieces of orange, pink and white gum in front of me, I struggled to decide which color to choose. Mom picked one for me so the attendant could move on to the next row. The gum was pink and I liked pink.

On the airplane everyone got a hot meal with real silverware and a miniature pack of Winston cigarettes. The stewardess could see we weren't adults but none of them bothered to remove the cigarettes before serving us. Society's view of smoking has come a long way. If we'd been flying to Detroit to visit our grandparents, we saved the cigarettes for Granddad Husen. I gave him the six miniature packs of cigarettes when we arrived at Grandma's house. He'd thank me and put them away where he stored the rest of his smoking paraphernalia. At age five, I didn't know I was actually killing him, instead of giving him a gift from the heart.

On this trip however, Granddad wasn't waiting for us at the other end of the flight and we didn't know we should be saving the cigarettes for anyone else. Dad smoked a cigar and we didn't yet know about June's love affair with cigarettes. I left mine on the tray. So did Steve. In those days flying was fun and full of freebies we were hesitant to leave behind.

Steve got the window seat and me, the middle. Observing the pecking order of siblings never deviated in anything we did in life. I spent the entire trip leaning across his lap in order to stare out the window. He didn't seem to mind. He was used to me pushing and shoving my way to the front of the pack. When we flew over the Grand Canyon, the stewardess pointed it out for us since we were such well-behaved children.

I didn't know what Steve felt about this trip or Dad and June. He didn't tell me. Being the only boy I recall both of my parents going out of their way to give him some different experiences. Once Dad took him on a father son trip to Cooperstown and the Baseball Hall of Fame. I wasn't allowed to go. Steve also had an elaborate toy slot car track set up in the basement and Mom took us to several organized races so he and his cars could participate. Bored watching cars go round and round on a track, I had to stand by and wait until the race finished.

He didn't tell me until we were adults that once he was playing with his cars, which were kept in a dark hidden corner of the basement laundry room of our big house. Mom and Dad came to the basement to have an argument so the kids wouldn't hear them upstairs. They didn't know Steve was listening on the other side of the wall. Mom used the word 'girlfriend' more than once. So Steve had some frame of reference about June that he never shared with his little sister even while confined for six hours on an airplane.

Dad retrieved us at the gate. These were the days when people walked freely from the check in desk to the gate and all points in between. He drove us home in relative silence since Steve and I were still engaged in staring out the window, gaping at the mountainous scenery surrounding the busy streets of this new city. We'd never been to the west coast before so seeing snow on the mountaintops in July went against everything we'd learned so far about the phenomenon of weather.

Dad and June's apartment, in a high rise building, was bright and spacious. I found it strange though to take an elevator to your front door. I was used to jumping out of the car and barreling through back door straight into the house. Elevators gave a different feel to being home by dragging out the comfort of finally arriving by navigating a maze of elevators and long hallways and saying a polite hello to strangers passed along the way.

Inside June waited with Mia, her dog, a miniature black poodle. Mia wagged her tail a bit and sniffed my ankles before trotting off to take a nap in a plush dog bed in the corner. I don't know how old Mia was at the time but it looked to me by the gray on her muzzle, like her best years were behind her.

We had a dog at home, Heidi, a miniature Schnauzer. A dog was another one of those things for my brother that my parents thought would be good for him. Only the dog was unruly, Steve had no idea how to train a puppy, and the rest of us had no interest in helping him. My parents told me from day one, she was Steve's dog, so he should be the one to walk her but he didn't. Heidi ended up being Mom's dog. No one could get close to Mom if Heidi was in the room. When we met Mia, neither of us knew that a dog could be loving and fun to play with, so we kept our distance.

I looked around at the furnishings that were so unlike anything my mother had purchased for our home. The oversized sofa covered in a gold vomit colored crushed velvet overpowered the room. An antique settee upholstered to match sat at an angle in the corner. Dad claimed an overstuffed armchair and ottoman in front of the television. I knew it belonged to him by the haphazard pile of newspapers on the floor next to it.

When Mom got tired of the sofa at home, she went out and bought a new slipcover. When it got dirty, she'd throw it in the washing machine and then tug and twist the shrunken fabric back onto the couch. The seat cushions turned up on the sides until we sat on them long enough to flatten them out. The skirt never quite made it back down to the floor and a ribbon of the old, original, white brocade underneath stuck out like a sore thumb.

"Don't sit on the settee," Dad instructed us. "It's old and fragile. And don't sit on those little chairs over there either." He pointed to two child-size chairs with carved wood backs and a peach colored velvet padded seat. I didn't plan on it anyway. Neither looked very comfortable for watching television.

The pictures on the walls were an eclectic mix of an abstract portrait whose mismatched eyes seemed to follow me around the room, a contemporary collection of sailboats and a painting of some odd and droopy orange flowers. At home we had paintings of Canadian geese, traditional landscapes and a barnyard scene complete with chickens and goats gracing the walls. I didn't find comfort or see the beauty in anything hanging here.

This home had a different smell to it too, kind of sweet and soapy. It reminded me of the scent of my father's shaving cream I came to know when I would sit in the bathroom and watch him shave in the morning. It wasn't just the bathroom that smelled that way here, it was the entire house. That scent left our home when Dad left, and here it overwhelmed me to the point I felt a little sick to my stomach.

The dishes in the kitchen and the towels hanging in the bathroom had an air of impracticability about them, frilly and embroidered. Fragile crystal bowls and china vases were scattered across the coffee table as well as the two large square end tables on either side of the puke colored sofa. Obviously, none of these things was geared to use and abuse by children. Nothing here had come from our house with Dad when he left. He brought nothing with him from our home. Even the clothes he wore looked different to me. I would be spending these three weeks in a foreign land.

At home I would spend the summer walking a mile to the Village Square shopping center to see what new stuff I could find at the drugstore. If there wasn't anything interesting there, I'd head down to Davis Bakery for an oversized chocolate chip cookie. On the weekends though, my best friend, Georgia, usually invited me to her family's cabin on a lake about two hours drive from home. I was already missing the hamburger cookouts, water skiing and being a part of a familiar family unit.

I met June only once before at the dinner Mom invited her to. As a shy and awkward pre-teen, I didn't kiss or hug her hello. Dad took our suitcases to the guest bedroom and June gave us a tour of the place so we didn't feel lost. Mia lay in her dog bed ignoring us.

Shortly after our arrival, June called me into her and Dad's bedroom. In her hand she had some round tubes wrapped in white paper.

"Linda, in case you need these, I keep them here in this drawer." She opened a dresser drawer and pointed to a box full of these tubes in the corner.

"What are they?" I asked.

"Tampons. In case you start your period while you're here," she said.

"Oh. Okay," I answered not wanting to reveal I had no idea where this conversation was headed.

I never saw a tampon before and didn't know what I was supposed to do with it. My mother bought me a thin, white elastic belt and showed me how to secure the ends of the bulky sanitary napkins, but I hadn't paid much attention. I don't believe they were packed in my suitcase for the trip here as a precautionary measure. Miss Larson, the health teacher had explained what would happen to us girls but I was convinced something this gross sounding would never happen to me.

June never had children of her own, so Mom must have called her in advance of my visit and asked her to watch out for me. That I was old enough to have a period would never cross my father's mind. He couldn't remember my birthday let alone my age. That's the way he was and all us kids became used to it at an early age. If June thought of it on her own, I'd be surprised. With no experience around children entering puberty, she couldn't possibly come up with the need for this conversation all by herself.

More likely is that the request from my mother was translated to June through my father.

"Junie, Sallie thinks Linny might start her period while she's here. Do you have some things for her to use if she does?" he asked. Junie was his nickname for June and Linny, for me.

"She can use some of mine." June answered.

If Mom mentioned pads versus tampons, Dad didn't retain that information to pass it along to June, or see it as necessary. He probably blocked out a lot of what Mom told him. June didn't go out and buy any special products suitable for a young girl, she shared her own.

As for me, I had no idea what on earth I would do with a tampon if the situation arrived. Thank God my period didn't start that summer and I was left to become a woman under my mother's instructions with bulky, uncomfortable super absorbent pads.

* * *

To keep us entertained for an extended period of time, Dad had a full schedule planned. Living in a city opened up a whole new world. We rode buses and trains, and took an elevator to the top of the Space Needle. The biggest thrill of all however, happened to be the indoor pool right on the first floor. If Dad would let us, Steve and I would spend the summer immersed in water. The community pool behind the local high school at home lacked the luxury we discovered downstairs.

Every morning after Dad left for work, June gave us each a beach towel and told us what time to be back upstairs. She didn't have a job while they lived in Seattle so I don't know what she did all day. Sending us off to swim by ourselves probably gave her a needed respite from active children. When we came back, she collected our towels, wet bathing suits and had sandwiches waiting on the dining room table with a smile. That was far more than our own mother could do between holding down a job and finding time to entertain children.

One Saturday afternoon, Dad announced we were all going for a ride on Sunday morning. He had a long history of packing us in the car to go for a ride. With no particular route in mind, he'd just drive. We only went along because one we had no choice in the matter and two, the ride always ended at the Dairy Queen for ice cream.

I hated these rides as he called them, mainly because as the youngest I got stuck in the middle on the bench seat in the front between him and Mom. He loved to smoke his cigar during these random trips around town causing me to throw up which grossed everybody out. Mom learned to come prepared with a paper bag and a bottle of Dramamine no matter how long or short the trip.

To this day I always need to know where I'm going when I get in a car. No surprises. I no longer have to come equipped with Dramamine but I can think of plenty of other more interesting things to do with my time than to drive mindlessly around looking at a new house being built, autumn leaves or some over the top Christmas light display. If I know I'm going to see those things, I'm all in but don't spring it on me after I've sat in the car for an hour going nowhere in particular. It's difficult to find a Dairy Queen these days.

"It's a surprise," Dad told us. "But you have to be ready early, by seven. We have reservations for breakfast at 8:30."

Steve and I figured we were going out for breakfast, which would be a real treat, but breakfast was somewhere very far away. Dad didn't usually start smoking a cigar until somewhere between lunch and dinner. I hoped I was safe from barfing in the back of his new Cadillac, because I'm sure no one filled June in on the Dramamine.

Steve and I were up, dressed and had the red sofa bed, which had been bought and squeezed into the tiny guest bedroom just for our visit, put away long before our departure time. We got the back seat of the Cadillac all to ourselves, Dad driving and June in the front passenger seat. We made our way out of the city and into the mountains and forest greenery full of tall, towering trees growing only inches apart. The road twisted and turned, curved and carved through the forest. I watched in amazement as the gorgeous scenery passed by.

"We're getting close," Dad would say periodically as we drove. "Are you hungry?"

"Yes!" we shouted out in unison.

The car pulled into the parking lot of the Snoqualmie Falls Lodge, a large log cabin like building nestled in the trees. I was intrigued. A cool breeze rustled the leaves and the smell of fresh pine reminded me of Christmas.

Dad parked the car and Steve and I ran to the entrance. Our shoes made a loud clumping noise on the wooden steps leading to the front porch crowded with rocking chairs. Inside, the mouth-watering aroma of bread baking, eggs frying and sausage sizzling filled my senses. My stomach rumbled loudly enough to be heard over the din of the crowded restaurant.

Once seated in the dining room, a young, cheerful waitress greeted us.

"You two have to order the pancakes! They're the best," she exaggerated for our benefit.

The only thing my mother knew how to make well was a blueberry pancake. I happen to come from a long line of women who don't know how to cook; it's in the genes. Mom made her famous pancakes every Sunday for lunch after church never using a recipe, all from memory. A cup of flour here, a pinch of salt there, sugar and an egg or two. They were to die for. No one twisted my arm to order pancakes if they were going to be even half as good as Mom's.

That's where Mom's culinary expertise ended, with pancakes. June however, loved to try new recipes she found in magazines while satisfying Dad's Midwest palate. She roasted a mean chicken, and osso bucco was often a Sunday treat. All her meals were served with lima beans, succotash or yellow wax beans that Dad loved. Steve and I hid those yucky vegetables under the bones so no one would notice we didn't eat them. June always served some kind of dessert, a store bought cake or pie, which we never got at home, or Dad took us out for ice cream.

I ordered the pancakes, sausage and orange juice. Steve ordered pancakes, bacon and apple juice because he had to be different. The happy waitress promptly delivered a huge stack of thick, golden brown pancakes. My mouth fell open at the sheer size of the plate now sitting in front of me.

Before I lifted my fork, the cheery server asked, "Would you like some syrup?" She held a gravy boat I guessed was full of some kind of local, sweet maple syrup.

"Yes, please." Who could eat pancakes without syrup?

With a small ladle, about the size of a quarter, on a long stainless steel handle, she scooped up the syrup, held it over her head before slightly tipping her hand and letting it drip down from at least three feet away onto my pancakes landing like a bull's-eye dead center before dribbling evenly over my stack of pancakes. I gasped.

She went to Steve and performed the same feat over his pancakes. I stared and gasped again. Dad and June laughed at our wide eyes and open mouths. On Sunday afternoons at home, syrup got squeezed out of a plastic bottle. I never saw it plummet from over my head and land exactly in the center of its intended target. I was going to try that at home, but Mom probably wouldn't allow it. I might miss without some practice, leaving a sticky mess on the rarely waxed dining room table.

After devouring our delicious syrup soaked breakfast, we walked over to see the Snoqualmie Falls. The falls drop 268 feet and are truly spectacular. They are higher than Niagara Falls, which I wouldn't see until much later in my life but I can still imagine the height of Snoqualmie Falls in my mind's eye. Snoqualmie Falls was my first viewing of an actual natural waterfall out in the world.

"Is the syrup drop supposed to match the waterfall?" I asked my Dad.

He chuckled. "I never thought of it that way, but I guess it does."

"No matter what it means, that was the best breakfast I've ever had," Steve, added to the conversation.

We watched the water pour over the mountain for quite a long time. I breathed in the fresh air and wondered what else of beauty the world had to offer me. June pointed out a bird in the trees she thought was an eagle but without Dad's binoculars that he'd left in the car, she couldn't be sure. We could hear the rat tat tat of a woodpecker off in the distance. A beautiful orange and black butterfly landed at my feet.

"Look June! Picnic tables," I said. "Can we come back again and have a picnic here? That would be so cool."

"Next week we're going to Mt. Rainier and I planned on packing lunch. I think you'll like that just as much as this," June said. "There you'll see snow in July."

"Snow? In summer?" Suddenly the world seemed a much bigger place full of new sights to explore. I loved watching the falls and now a mountain called my name.

I've traveled around the world since that day at the falls and often I think my love affair with distant places began here. The travel bug bit me and me alone, none of the rest of my siblings. There's not a place in the world I'd refuse to go if the opportunity presented itself. I have a pancake and a waterfall to thank.

In later years every time I planned for an overseas trip, June would ask, "Can you send me a postcard?"

"Of course I will," I'd say.

I dated the postcard and she noted the date it arrived in her mailbox. The number of days it took for the mail to arrive from some far away land was a favorite topic of conversation. She saved every postcard I sent, organizing them in a photo album she wrote my name on. Paris, Rome, China, Rio de Janeiro. I'd been around the world and June came with me.

At Snoqualmie Falls I began to warm up to this person who had unexpectedly inserted herself into my life. She let us go swimming whenever we liked for as long as we wanted. June never stopped us from having a second scoop of ice cream for dessert. She giggled at our wide-eyed wonder of new places, and seemed to enjoy finding different experiences to keep us entertained. June picked the places she thought we'd like and Dad drove. Dad smiled at June and she batted her eyelashes back. I figured she was here to stay.

"You may encounter many defeats, but you must not be defeated." – Maya Angelou

CHAPTER EIGHT

That first full day left me exhausted. I'd never been a high-energy kind of person so it didn't take much for me to reach my limit. Richard had the energy. He was always in motion, cooking, cleaning, and washing. If he wasn't moving, I knew he didn't feel well. He gave me plenty of time to read a book or work on my writing so I consider myself very lucky. Richard would have June's apartment cleaned out and sold before I could empty the trash even once. But this was my job. I wouldn't even think of asking him to help me. He had done this task for his own parents and now it was my turn to do it for mine.

I still had one more task before I could go back to my hotel and crawl into bed. Visit June. By now I knew the route through the lobby to the elevator, up to the third floor and to the far end of the hall. For a person so uneasy on her feet, this is the worst possible room we could choose for her. Time wasn't on our side and this room was available immediately, so I grabbed it. In my exhausted state, it was a hike even for me. The door to her room was propped wide open, the television blaring. The other residents must be deaf if they weren't complaining about the noise. I didn't bother to knock; no one would hear me. `

June lay on her bed curled up in the fetal position, her eyes closed. A slight grin graced her lips. She looked peaceful for a change. Not wanting to wake her I sat down in the chair in the corner to wait. She sensed the presence of someone else in the room.

"Linda! Where have you been?" she yelled out in a gravely voice.

"You were sleeping. I've been right here," I said.

I know that's a lie but I was beginning to understand how to answer her to cause the least amount of agitation. I wouldn't always succeed but I was giving it my best shot.

"I. Want. To. Go. Home," she screamed at me.

Dad never allowed yelling in the house. It startled me whenever she raised her voice this loud.

"June. This is your home now," I answered. "See. There's your favorite painting." I pointed toward a lovely still life of autumn leaves and branches. It had hung in a prominent place over the couch in every home she lived in as long as I could remember.

June's eyes darted around the room. Her gaze turned dark and blank as she studied the picture of my father on her nightstand, before moving onto the antique stained glass lamp she inherited from her aunt on the desk.

"How did I end up in this little bed?" she complained. "I hate it. I'm afraid I'm going to fall out."

The management at the assisted living home insisted we buy a new mattress. A used one was unacceptable plus her king size bed wouldn't fit in this tiny room. Bed bugs, they told me. Richard called in a favor after his long career in the furniture business and we bought her a brand new twin bed with a matching dresser and two nightstands. The furniture was gorgeous, well built and at a bargain price.

I thought she'd like to have something new. How wrong I'd been. She didn't want to give up anything, not even her old and lumpy king bed with a nicked and wobbly wooden headboard.

"I hate this bed." She pounded her fists into the mattress.

"June. Give yourself some time to get used to it." My frustration at this conversation grew exponentially each time she announced her rebuttal, my guilt grew heavier, and my sadness forced me to hold back tears.

"I want a cigarette," she said.

"Okay. Let's go downstairs and get them from the receptionist. I'll sit with you outside and we'll chat." I went to the side of her bed to help her up.

"No!" she screamed. "I don't want to go outside. I want to smoke it here."

"June, you know the rules. You can't smoke in your room. Yvette has your cigarettes downstairs and you can ask for them anytime you want."

"No! Go get them for me," she insisted.

"June, you know I can't do that," I answered in as soft and soothing tone as I could muster, my annoyance at her multiplying.

"I hate it here. I want to go home." Like a child throwing a temper tantrum, her face scrunched up into a thousand more wrinkles than her aging skin already showed and turned a bright shade of crimson.

"June. I'm sorry you're so upset but this is the best thing for you." I reached for her hand. "I want you to be safe and you weren't safe in your apartment."

Tears ran down her cheek, which she dabbed with a tissue she always kept wadded up in her hand. June and her tissue went together like peanut butter and jelly. She would never be without one in her hand or tucked up her sleeve.

Playtime with all of her dogs over the years included a game where they nuzzled her hand until she allowed the corner of her tissue into view. Shana would tear off a piece and enjoy eating it like a snack. Watching this totally grossed me out, the dog eating a snotty tissue, but June loved it. She smiled with her soft, signature giggle every time the dog asked to play.

When Steve and his wife, Karen married, Dad and June went on a well remembered and often discussed drinking binge. We knew them to love a few drinks but starting with champagne in the afternoon before moving on to glass after glass of vodka seemed excessive for them. After the reception ended, a group of us sat in the bar while the two of them each downed many more glasses of vodka, their drink of choice. In fact the rest of us left them in the hotel bar well after midnight, we'd had our fill. Dad insisted they weren't ready to go.

I have no idea how many more drinks they had or if they had any trouble finding their room that night, but when I saw them the next morning at breakfast, Dad claimed he didn't have a hangover and June held a tissue to her weeping eye where it remained for the rest of the day. She insisted she wasn't crying or teary about the wedding and didn't know what was causing this but the tears continued to flood from her eye. Together we came to the conclusion all that vodka needed an escape. Out of her tear duct it came. Thank goodness June came equipped with a supply of white tissues. She went through an entire box that day.

I brought her a new box of Kleenex from the bathroom and set it on her nightstand. She grabbed another one without looking at me.

"Linda."

I knew I was in trouble when she said my name in certain way with hard inflection on the last syllable.

"You tell them I want dinner in my room. I refuse to go to the dining room," her body stiffened as she spoke.

"Why don't you want to go to the dining room?' This was worse than trying to reason with a child.

"You tell them I'm sick. I'm not going," June insisted. "You tell them."

"The nurse will come take your temperature," I said. "She'll know you're lying."

"You tell them." June gritted her teeth.

I kissed her on the forehead. "I'll tell them. I'm going to go. I'll see you tomorrow."

"I love you. Don't forget to tell them," June said, her tone softening.

"Love you too. Bye bye." I turned away and left the room.

I tracked down the nurse on my way out. June needed a long list of things attended to that had been neglected for a long time. She needed to see the podiatrist, the doctor and the hairdresser. God forbid I forget the hairdresser; she'd never speak to me again.

"June wants to have dinner in her room," I said with a wink knowing already what her answer would be.

"Residents are not allowed to be served meals in their room unless they're sick," she responded in a matter of fact tone.

"I understand. She's pretty miserable and wants a cigarette badly," I said.

The nurse rolled her eyes at me. "She needs to quit."

"I understand but she's been smoking since she was a teenager and now she's 91. Can the doctor give her something to help with the nicotine withdrawal?" I asked politely.

"I'll check with him," she answered curtly.

"Thank you," I replied with a similar edge to my voice.

I learned quickly, it was important to June's well being I kiss these people's asses. There is no way to sugar coat that phrase when it comes to taking care of the elderly. While they are keeping track of how much food she eats and her urine output, secretly they are also marking on a tally sheet who visits and how often. If that number doesn't add up to a total the nurse deems an acceptable level, watch out. Your loved one will be labeled as neglected and no matter how hard you try to change their perception, it will never happen. Another layer of thick gooey butter cream frosting disguised as guilt had been spread on the cake and a heaping forkful shoveled in my mouth.

I'm grateful for the nurses and aides who chose this way to make a living. I could never do it, and as a society we need them. As more baby boomers retire, we will need even more trained medical workers. Families are mobile and distant from loved ones and are either unable or unwilling to care for their parents. So they get shipped off to the assisted living facility on the way to the full-fledged nursing home. I'm a fool if I don't think the resident who came in here with the fanciest jewelry and brought it even after they'd been told not to, gets the best treatment. I can say thank you with a smile, but I really need to send over a tray of cookies and sign June's name to the card when I get home.

Deflated once again by the nurse's quick answers to my questions, I wondered what had happened to the kind and compassionate attention the staff assured me of when I shopped for assisted living homes. I made the decision to move June here with my nose instead of my head. This place didn't stink of pee and old people like the others. There was a jam-packed calendar of activities June would never participate in and they had the all-important beauty salon. When I picked Hawthorne I never thought to interview the nurse to see if she had a personality.

I fell into bed drained of my last ounce of energy and yet sleep refused to come. My only wish that night was to be able to sit down next to June, hand her a cigarette and a glass of vodka and have our usual laughs over a conversation about nothing. I tossed and turned with worry until the sun came up the next morning.

"Givers have to set limits, because takers rarely do." – Irma Kurtz

CHAPTER NINE

Today I arrived at the apartment armed with plug in air fresheners hoping to keep my cigarette smoke headache from returning. Maybe I would be exchanging it for a perfume headache since I was highly allergic to scents too, but it couldn't be any worse than how I felt yesterday. Every outlet in the living room now sported a fancy flower shaped plug in air freshener. I still however, resisted the urge to breath deeply until they had a chance to work their air freshening magic. June would insist her apartment smelled clean and fresh as a rose. She'd become nose blind to the smell of her cigarettes.

After scouring the Internet, I found a service to help me sell the furniture and get the apartment ready for sale, *A Time to Move*. Barbara was due to arrive at ten o'clock to assess the situation and estimate a price. The money again. I found myself taking over where June left off.

She constantly worried about her money, saying she was a product of the Depression of the 1930's. Now that her mind couldn't remember anything about finances, she passed that worry on to me. I couldn't move the antique china cabinet containing the Waterford crystal or the 1960's Mediterranean bedroom set I remembered from their apartment in Seattle. They were both old and worn and weighed a ton. Solid wood. Dressers weren't made that way any more.

I had to spend her money for my own sanity. Let's just hope I could do it reasonably and leave something for her Depends. Adult diapers were another item I never in my wildest dreams thought I would have to pay attention too. They are just another check mark on the bucket list of necessary but unpleasant things that are part of growing old. The Hawthorne Residence added them to her monthly rent to the tune of an extra one hundred dollars.

Barbara arrived right on time and I gave her a tour. When we were done, which didn't take long, she sat at the dining room table and did some figuring. She gave me what I thought was a fair price to move what was left of the furniture, donate to charity anything left and clean the place including all the appliances to have it ready for sale. I heaved a huge sigh of relief and signed the contract.

"I know a man who deals in antiques and might want to look at some of these pieces," Barbara offered. "Whatever he wants to take to auction, you can work out the details with him. Is it alright if I call him for you?"

June always thought the antiques she inherited from her aunt were worth a fortune. I had a more down to earth view on the subject. Richard was left a houseful of his mother, Floss' flea market finds. As a weekend trip and a way to entertain young children, she packed the kids in the car and drove to Amish country from their home outside of Philadelphia. Richard and his brother climbed under the tables, crawled through the grass and smeared the soot from antique flatirons across their faces. Every now and then Floss would snap a photograph to save their antics for posterity. She, however, was really looking for ways to inexpensively furnish a home.

When Floss died we ended up with an Amish corner cupboard with all original glass complete with bubbles and swirls and a hole where supposedly a mouse chewed his way in, a large wood desk with lots of secret compartments and a ladies writing desk with inlaid mother of pearl. Beautiful pieces, but when we tried to sell them, there were no takers. Smaller living spaces mean more efficient and multiple uses for furniture.

I hadn't researched June's pieces like I had Floss' but I suspected a similar outcome. We now lived in an age of cell phones and iPads. We read books online, no need for a bookcase. We eat out far more often than we eat in. Fancy cut crystal stemware and gold-rimmed china are best seen in a museum. I was hopeful but tried not to be too optimistic about the amount of money I could raise from their sale.

June had already reached the ripe, old age of 91 before needing any additional care. The odds were against her outliving her money but I had to guard her money as if she'd live to be 110. She was after all a life long smoker and drinker who'd gotten this far with no serious health issues.

Within minutes Roger knocked on the front door. Now, I like to think I'm a pretty good judge of character and Barbara seemed to be a kind, compassionate and honest person. Her business focused on helping elderly people transition from what they find familiar into a different phase of their life. That Roger showed up so swiftly made me suspicious she had him waiting in the wings, ready to pounce on an overwhelmed and unsuspecting me.

He carefully examined the china cabinet, then moved on to the dining room table and Andrew Wyeth prints hanging on the living room wall. In the kitchen, he opened every drawer and cabinet studying the stainless steel flatware with a curved handle and a tiny rose in the center or the chipped and cracked, well used blue and white Spode dinner plates. Whenever I came to visit, I ate off of them, washed them and put them back in the cupboard. I didn't want the plates, they'd seen better days, but the picture of the girl at the well had been etched into my memory.

All of June's possessions were old, used long after their useful life had ended. At least in my mind they had, but not June's. That served to explain the difference in our generations. Hers held on to their toasters and refrigerators having them repaired when they broke down. I, on the other hand, belonged to the disposable generation. Repairs to my washing machine cost over $300, a new machine only $600. The choice to buy new for me was easy. Her depression era upbringing of frugality had never left her.

Over the years, after my father died, I tried to help her with her money. She never wanted to listen to me, that was her stubborn side. When she moved into the condo, she signed up for a very expensive appliance maintenance plan. She paid for the soup to nuts plan she insisted would buy her a new appliance if any of hers broke down and could no longer be fixed. What June never understood is the repairman would use chewing gum to fix a hose in the dishwasher if he had to, just so the company would never replace a single appliance in her kitchen.

She had blue plastic ice cube trays in the freezer because the ice-maker in the refrigerator never worked and the appliance maintenance plan for some unknown reason excluded the icemaker. She convinced herself she didn't need it fixed; she enjoyed big, homemade cubes in her vodka better. It drove me nuts every time I had to twist those hard frozen trays. I wondered how June could do it with her small, arthritic hands.

Roger spoke in a long drawn out southern drawl. "I can sell most of this at auction. I'll take it to my warehouse in Tennessee. People love stuff like this up there. Whatever I get for it, you get half. I'll move it all out of here for you." He paused. "My truck's downstairs."

Still suspicious at the fast speed at which things were now moving, "Do you have a contract or anything for me to sign? How do I know you'll send me the money?"

Barbara piped in. "I've been doing business with Roger for years. I wouldn't recommend him if he didn't have good character."

"I'll come tomorrow morning early, bring the contract and load my truck." He extended his hand to me.

We shook on it. I couldn't waste any more time comparing prices or waiting for another estate appraisal. If Roger sent the money, great. If he didn't, I probably wouldn't lose enough to make much of a difference to June's future well being. If I made the wrong decision trusting Roger, then so be it. Lesson learned. I wanted badly to stop worrying about things I couldn't control and start trusting the good people in this world who were willing to help me.

When Barbara and Roger left, I gathered my things and locked the door behind me. Tomorrow would come soon enough. It was time for my afternoon visit with June.

"Love does not consist of gazing at each other, but in looking together in the same direction." - Antoine de Saint-Exupery

CHAPTER TEN

The following summer Steve and I again flew out to Seattle for our three weeks of required visitation. With our suitcases loaded in the trunk of the Ford my father left behind and my mother still drove, we made the hour long drive to the Cleveland airport.

Ten minutes into our journey, Mom started on her usual lecture on how we were to behave while in the care of our father.

"Be sure to brush your teeth. Toothpaste and your toothbrushes are in the pouch in the side of your suitcase," she started. "And wash your face before you go to bed."

"Yes, Mom," I said annoyed that she thought I didn't know how to do something I did every day.

"Do what your father tells you. June too. No backtalk out of either of you," she said.

Steve and I didn't know how to talk back. Why Mom would even use those words to us made no sense. She knew we knew better but needed an excuse in the off chance Dad called her to tell her we were misbehaving. Our Midwest upbringing made sure that we never voiced our opinion no matter what the circumstance and especially not to a parent. In our world, adults were in charge and not to be messed with. The penalty was much worse than any pleasure gathered by a stupid childish rebuttal.

Dad and June had moved to a new apartment, in a smaller building but without a pool and a fitness room. At first glance we wondered how we would be spending our time while Dad worked during the day without the benefit of a swimming pool.

Inside the apartment were two new dogs, Maggie and Molly. Maggie was a gray miniature poodle with a curly coat and a craving for food of any kind. Molly, a toy poodle, was tiny and cuddly and gave kisses nonstop. Immediately we found two new friends in a new place. I didn't ask what happened to Mia.

The red sofa bed waited for us in the den. We were starting to feel at home with things around us seemingly more familiar than they'd been last summer. All of June's knickknacks, while last year seemed new and strange, now gave me a sense of belonging. The crystal slipper now sat on an end table next to the sofa, and a round, floral Limoges box had taken its place on the coffee table. The sudsy scent remained the same at the new apartment as if it came from an aerosol can.

The one thing I noticed that I hadn't paid any attention to the last summer was that this had become Dad's home. He was comfortable here, his cigar box just within reach of his favorite chair, newspapers waited for him to read them, crackers in the cupboard exactly where he knew to find them when he needed a snack. Dad appeared more at home than I remember him being in the rare times he spent with us in our big house in Cleveland. He left our family and our home taking nothing with him to his new life. No photos of his children, none of his books that lined the shelves of our living room, or even his piano that he loved to play belting out a popular song of the sixties, *Alley Cat* every time he came home. I think he liked it this way.

Our lives went on, school, girl scouts, church. Dad called every couple weeks and I had to stop whatever I was doing when the phone rang. It didn't matter if I was doing homework or eating dinner. The conversations were short, he asked questions and I gave one or two word answers. The call ended the same way every time with Dad's quip that I'd grown tired of long ago.

"Stay out of the pool hall, Linny." he said.

He didn't miss us and we had stopped missing him a long time ago.

* * *

We'd been in Seattle for more than a week and had settled into a routine. Dad went to work, and we watched some game shows on television. No one seemed to care what we watched, at least we hadn't been informed of any 'no Three Stooges' rule but as hard as we tried we couldn't find the illicit show on any channel.

After lunch when only soap operas were on, Steve and I went swimming. Yes, swimming. The apartment building was built on pilings over water. I'm not sure what water but some finger or inlet of Puget Sound. Along side the building, ran a wooden dock. Steve and I raced out to the end and jumped off. The water so deep we never touched the bottom. Waves from the wake of a passing boat let us bobble up and down in the water with little effort. This was even better than the heated indoor swimming pool we inhabited last summer. Steve and I would paddle and putz around in the water until we ran out of energy. Then we'd sun ourselves on the dock until June came down with the dogs in tow to get us for dinner.

One morning Dad came to the breakfast table in his casual clothes, a pair of sans a belt trousers and loose fitting cotton shirt. Something would be different today but I had no idea why.

"I'm taking June to the dentist today. She has to have some teeth pulled," he said. "No swimming while we're gone."

"Okay. How long will you be gone?" We'd never been left alone in this apartment before even though we were almost teenagers.

"We should be home by lunchtime. I'll call if it's later. June made sandwiches if you get hungry," he said.

A nervous June and my just as nervous but attentive father walked out the door hand in hand. Steve and I parked ourselves on the red sofa; each with a dog tucked under an arm and watched some mindless daytime television show. It would be a long day without some swimming to fill the time.

"Have you ever noticed anything weird about her teeth before?" I asked Steve.

"No. Have you? She doesn't have bad breath but I never got close enough to smell it," he answered.

"They must be gross if she's having all of them pulled out," I said.

"They must really be yucky." Steve scrunched up his nose.

"Why would she make an appointment to have them pulled while we're here anyway? We're going home in less than a week," I wondered.

"Maybe Dad didn't tell her we were coming." Steve remarked. "Take door number two," he shouted at Monty Hall and a contestant dressed as a devil with a pitchfork on *Let's Make A Deal.*

With not much to occupy our time except the television, we ate the sandwiches well before noon. Dad guided June through the front door around 2 p.m., holding her elbow, the same way he led her out this morning. But this time, he took her straight into their bedroom and shut the door. When he finally came out, I peeked through the crack in the door. The room was dark and all the curtains were drawn.

"Don't bother Junie," he said to us. He sat in his chair in the living room and read the Women's Wear Daily.

By this time we were glued to the afternoon soap operas. Around five o'clock, Dad stuck his head into the den.

"Hungry?" he asked. "Junie's sleeping so don't make any noise."

Steve and I both nodded in agreement. We put on our shoes, turned off the TV and tiptoed to the front door. We followed Dad through the hallways, into the elevator and down to the parking garage to his Cadillac.

"Chinese food sound good?" Dad asked.

Whether it did or not, we answered yes. Chinese was his favorite and that's what we were having. McDonald's was on the tip of my tongue but I didn't dare say it. I doubt Mickey D's was on Dad's list of acceptable eateries. Steve would have preferred a milkshake and a hamburger too, but we knew the Chinese restaurant menu by heart and what to order before we even got there. Dad never questioned what we ordered. Shrimp in lobster sauce with some fried rice and egg roll on the side. Fortune cookies for dessert.

We didn't bring home any of the leftovers for June and we didn't see or hear a peep from her for the rest of the night. In fact June remained holed up in the bedroom for the next few days. Dad didn't need help finding restaurants to take us out for breakfast, lunch and dinner. He had a favorite diner we frequented often and of course the Chinese restaurant, always capped off with a trip to the ice cream store.

June finally reappeared to make us Dad's favorite pot roast the night before we were to go back home. We both would have preferred to have Chinese again rather than the detested pot roast.

"It's your going away dinner," she announced. June looked the same to me. I didn't notice anything different about her new teeth but I guess the old ones had been swapped out for a new set.

We ate while trying to look like we enjoyed it. At least we both knew we wouldn't get pot roast at home. Mom stopped making it once Dad left. We also wouldn't get the trip to the ice cream parlor that followed the pot roast either. There were trade offs no matter which parent had control of us.

Steve grew three inches during those three weeks, able to look straight into Dad's eyes by the time we left but Dad never noticed. Mom complained how fat we both were when she picked us up at the airport. Dad had not a clue that he had overfed his children either. It was simply the summer of June's teeth or her new dentures, whatever way I wanted to look at it.

Dad and June were a single unit, a team of their own, and they didn't want anyone else to join in order to be happy. We certainly weren't neglected as children but our parents focused on their own needs, not on ours. Steve and I were given what they thought we needed without asking what we were actually interested in. So when June had to schedule the appointment for her new teeth, Dad never said, "Can you wait until the kids go home?" His world revolved around only June and she came first in his life.

"Every day may not be good,
But there is something good in
every day."

CHAPTER ELEVEN

"Susan. The nurse from Hawthorne called me five times about her shoes," I said.

A roar of laughter pummeled through the phone into my ear. I moved the phone away until it stopped. Standing in Wal-Mart staring at a wall of footwear, I decided to call Susan for advice. Apparently I wasn't going to get the kind of sibling support I was searching for.

June had a hammertoe. The long second toe on her right foot curled across her big toe. I can only assume for the majority of her working years, she had crammed her feet into ill fitting high heels all while walking mile after mile every working day as she combed the department store floors or pounded the New York City pavement on a buying trip.

No matter how much nudging I did over the years, she refused to have the toe corrected. Mom declined to take prescribed medicine for high blood pressure and that choice cost her dearly cutting her life short. I'm sure the toe caused a lot of unnecessary pain over the years. The lesson learned from the two most prominent women in my life for my own later years is to never skip a doctor's appointment and if it's broken get it fixed. There is no need to suffer thanks to today's modern medicine.

Our family was first introduced to the toe on a trip to Disney World. For some unknown reason, we had come together in an attempt to act like a family and gathered at Disney World for a week's vacation. The year was 1988. Susan, Greg and their son Luke came from Ohio along with Steve and Karen. Martha and Tom came with a combination of children, some his, some hers and one who didn't belong to either of them. Dad and June and Richard and I drove to Orlando in separate cars. We decided we might need Dad's roomy Cadillac to pack a few more people into in case we decided to drive somewhere and not rely on the hotel bus.

I bought Dad a Donald Duck hat at the Disney store in the mall and gave it to him for his birthday a few weeks before we were scheduled to leave. He wore it all day every day we were on vacation, to the pool, on a trek around one of the theme parks, at dinner and with cocktails. He stood out in the crowd with Donald's big yellow duckbill sticking out and his oversized eyes topped by his bright blue sailor hat on Dad's large frame. His favorite pink, white and blue plaid polyester sans a belt trousers completed the outlandish outfit he loved but embarrassed the rest of us.

Dad wanted to make us laugh. He wanted to impress Mickey that he too could let his hair down and have a good time in the happiest place on Earth. I often thought he was trying to make up for lost time having never taken us away on a vacation. As kids we went to visit him wherever he lived at the time. Sure we were leaving home for a time but he wasn't. We were his guests subject to his rules. Here in Disney World, Mickey and Minnie set the rules.

On the last night we all went to the luau at the Polynesian Hotel, he and June lagged far behind the rest of us when we were making our way back to the bus stop. We only had one more day left of our family time together and everyone was tired, even the kids, who in the eyes of the rest of us had boundless energy. All that hula dancing made my eyes heavy and my feet feel as if I was wearing a pair of concrete boots. When I arrived at the bus stop and the Donald Duck hat wasn't visible in the crowd, I had a feeling something was amiss.

I slowly labored down the long and winding pathway retracing my steps and found Dad and June sitting on a bench taking a rest.

"Are you guys all right?" I asked.

"June's toe is bothering her," Dad said.

Her toe?

"Do you have a blister? I've got band aids back at the hotel," I said. A prepared traveler, a portion of my suitcase was always set aside for aspirin, Pepto Bismol, Neosporin and a variety of other pharmaceuticals just in case. I loved to travel and never wanted a blister or a bout of diarrhea to interrupt my adventure. I carried enough for everyone with me.

June took off her right shoe and rubbed her foot.

"I don't think it's a blister," she said squinting while trying to focus in the pale lamplight.

That's when I saw it. Her second toe crossed over on top of her big toe. My first thought was "Why don't you get that fixed?" but I knew such a comment would not be well received. She hiked all over Disney World in shoes that didn't fit since appearances always trumped comfort and with only the benefit of nine toes to steady her, no wonder she was in pain.

Dad held June's hand and I stayed close by on the slow walk to catch up with the others.

"What's the matter?" my sister asked as we came into view.

"June's toe is bothering her," Dad answered.

"Her toe?" Susan said, not really asking a question but making a comment.

I stood behind them waving my hand and shaking my head to signal not to ask anymore questions. The sight of "the toe" traumatized me and I feared having nightmares of it chasing me through my usually pleasant dreams.

After that incident and for as long as I could remember she only ever wore these funny little sandals with a cork wedge heel and a black leather strap with a silver buckle across the top. June swore these were the most comfortable shoes ever and wore nothing else. At least twenty-five identical pairs of black Worishofer slip ons littered her closet floor. Where she found them, I'll never know but they are probably the only footwear on earth that left enough room for the pesky twisted toe.

Somehow she convinced the old lady shoe store in downtown Delray Beach to get the sandals for her. June bought a lot of them because the salesman would happily make a house call bringing the order directly to her apartment. Once she went to Susan's in Dayton, Ohio for Christmas. It was 20 degrees outside with a foot of snow atop a layer of ice. June wore only a pair of her favorite sandals and knee-high nylon hose, insisting for the entire trip her feet weren't cold.

June had only been in her new room at Hawthorne for a few days when the phone calls about the shoes started.

"She's going to fall in those shoes. They don't give her any support." The nurse spoke to me like I must be an idiot to let on old woman walk around in a pair of ill-fitting cork sandals.

"What do you suggest she wear?" I asked.

"She needs something that will support her ankle, like a sneaker. Something with a rubber sole," the nurse said.

"I think that will rub on the crazy toe she has. How can I get around it?" I had the shoe conversation with June many times to no avail. Now she was in new and strange surroundings, going through nicotine withdrawal and as mad as hornet at me for doing all this to her. Now would be a good a time as any to fit her into a new pair of footwear.

The nurse offered this advice. "Get a wide width and half size bigger. Velcro is better than laces." The nurse again displayed no compassionate bedside manner but she spoke knowledgeably of old people and their shoes.

At Wal-Mart shoes are hung on a peg-board display. No boxes neatly stacked in rows like in the kind of store June would prefer to frequent. Pairs of sneakers were held together with a plastic tag and a hook. I stood before them trying to pick out a style June might like, while waiting for my sister to stop laughing.

"And who's going to put these shoes on her feet?" Susan asked.

"I guess I've been elected. Unless you want to get on a plane and come down for the fun." Who the hell did she think was going to do it?

"Woo. That's a good one." Susan continued to giggle. "I'll say she's about the same as me, a seven and a half or an eight."

"OK. And I have to get it bigger to accommodate the toe." Over the years the toe had become a living, breathing entity all on its own.

Scanning the wall, I searched for the eights. "What color do you think I should get? White or white?"

The only choice I had was some big, clunky orthopedic white sneakers with Velcro straps. In comparison to her beloved sandals, no matter how I delivered these shoes, it was going to be a very hard sell.

"White sounds good," Susan chuckled.

"Any tips on how I should get these monstrosities on her feet?" I asked wanting more pity than advice.

"Wait until it's about time for dinner. When the aide comes to take her downstairs she won't be able to keep arguing with you. You know those old people, their day revolves around the next meal," she answered. "At 4:30 she'll be hungry. They have feeding at those places down to a science."

"I hope you're right. Wish me luck." To be on the safe side, I grabbed a size eight and an eight and a half from the wall and gathered myself together to be ready for an ensuing battle.

A Bittersweet Goodnight

I pulled into the parking lot of the now familiar Hawthorne Residence. Gathering up all my bags of goodies, I headed inside. Yvette, the receptionist, or concierge as she called herself, stopped me.

"Did you order the newspaper for Mom?" she asked.

June always enjoyed having a daily newspaper. She read it slowly, making it last all day until it was time to turn on the television. She prided herself in not turning on the TV until it was time for the evening newscast. I never understood what was wrong with watching a little *Dr. Phil, Maury,* or *The Price is Right* during the day. She might have gotten a laugh or two out of it. But no. The newspaper kept her busy in between her precisely planned cigarette breaks.

"I did. Is it not being delivered?" I asked.

"It's not that. She's not interested in it, can't concentrate on it. It's going to waste. You can cancel it if you'd like," Yvette said.

"Thanks for letting me know." I wanted June to feel at home but I should have suspected this when I found the pile of newspapers strewn across the floor of her living room. She probably hadn't been reading it for a long time but wanted to continue the impression she did. She tricked me once again. I held the power to upset the precarious routine she so carefully constructed in order to stay home. June's plan miserably failed.

I found June's door propped open. On tiptoes, I tried not to wake her but her eyes burst open with the rustling of my bags. I brought bottled water, cheese and crackers, a box of tissues, a wall calendar and some pencils she liked for doing crossword puzzles. If she wasn't reading the newspaper, she most likely wasn't doing her puzzles either.

She might be nice to me today if I showed her these items and they triggered in her mind that her charade continued.

Oh, and of course, I almost forgot, the shoes. The stylish and attractive shoes, June was going to love without a doubt slipped out of the plastic bag and onto the floor. I couldn't keep them a secret any longer.

June lay in bed looking at me with indifference as I showed off my purchases.

"Look cheese and crackers!" I exclaimed. "You can have a snack. The cheese is all sliced, ready for whenever you want some." June used to love nibbling on cheese and crackers with her cocktail every evening but since she no longer had access to vodka she might not want it.

June rolled in her weathered lips and glared in my direction.

"I'll put it in the fridge with a few bottles of water," I said.

The glaring continued.

I took a deep breath, steeling my body and mind for what was about to happen. Now was the time for the shoes.

"June, the nurse says you must have new shoes." I diverted the blame to someone else so I might have a chance of getting through the next few minutes unscathed.

"I don't want new shoes," she yelled while pounding her fists into the bed.

"I'm sorry. You don't have a choice." I opened the dresser drawer looking for the socks Susan bought for her. "Let's put some socks on first."

"No! I don't want any," she cried.

I sat on the edge of the bed, rolled up a sock and tried to slip it gently on the squirming foot. I had made a conscious decision not to have children of my own, and now my decision I made all those years ago was confirmed. All this fiddling around arguing left me weary. I found it hard enough to keep my own life in order and now I had to do it for June too. In my brain she was an adult, a friend, a stubborn but kind woman. Here and now lay a child in a worn and wrinkled body. All the wisdom of age trapped inside only to be seen in rare and fleeting moments when all the channels clicked back into place, sometimes for a minute and sometimes for ten, just long enough to fool even the smartest of onlookers.

Socks firmly in place, it was time for the shoes. I ripped open the Velcro straps and stretched the shoes apart forcing the right shoe to open as wide as I could make it.

"I want my sandals. Those are ugly. I won't wear them," she said.

"Wait until you walk in them. You are going to love them, June." I did my best to sound encouraging.

Gently I held her foot and gave it a little massage to relax it. I slid the sneaker over the crooked toe. I wiggled her heel into place.

" Owwww!" June squeaked. "Oww!"

I quickly got it off. Too small. Thank goodness I bought two different sizes. For once in this whole process I thought ahead. Smart me. The larger size slid on easily and there was no yelping with pain.

"There you go. Don't you look stylish?" I said.

"I look like an idiot. Take them off. Take them off now, Linda." I'm not sure how to describe the look on her face. Pale, desperate, frightened, all of the above and more. All I wanted for her was to be able to rip off these horrid things, give her back the shoes she loved, wave a magic wand and put everything back to the way it once was.

"C'mon. Let's go for a walk," I urged with a quiver in my voice while I pushed back tears I hoped June couldn't detect.

"Get me my walker," June answered.

Right then, I stopped. Her walker? Several years ago the doctor recommended June would benefit from the use of a walker. It would help her be less afraid and more stable on her feet. She complied, had Ted, her driver, take her to the medical supply store, purchased the walker and then parked it in the corner of the dining room to collect dust. Only old people use walkers she told me.

"Miss June. It's time for dinner." A cheerful voice chimed from the doorway.

I glanced at my watch. It said 4:15. The early bird special was alive and well at the Hawthorne Assisted Living Residence.

June's walker never moved an inch the entire time it resided in her condo. Now it was making up for lost time. I moved it in front of her, held on to it while she used it for support and stood up. Off we went. New shoes and a walker and she was ready to run marathon.

I breathed a sigh of relief before chasing her down the hall and into the elevator.

"These shoes are comfortable. I like them." June looked at me with a smile peeking out between the wrinkles.

"You like them?" I asked in disbelief.

"It's easy to walk in them. I love them," she smiled.

My mouth fell open. Right then and there I wondered why I gave up drinking after moving away. June always had a cocktail in hand, ready to raise it in a toast for any little reason. Without her encouragement to refill my glass on pace with hers, I have since come to the realization I didn't need alcohol to make me more interesting or appealing. But if June accepted these new shoes back then, we would have celebrated with one helluva party.

"Behold the turtle. He makes progress only when he sticks his neck out."
— James Conant

CHAPTER TWELVE

Roger, his wife and daughter waited in the parking lot when I arrived the next morning. I helped them carry some packing boxes and we chatted easily on the way to the fifth floor. Sarah, Roger's wife, who was tall and lean with graying hair wrapped up in a bun at the nape of her neck, complained about the Florida heat. Their daughter, Tina walked with a slight limp. She chose her words carefully when she spoke and displayed a curiosity about who I was and to whom all the furniture belonged. Tina appeared to be in her thirties but had a vocabulary of a ten year old.

As promised, Roger brought the contract and we both signed it. He handed me a copy and gave the remaining pages to Sarah, who filed them in a manila folder marked with my name.

"There are some knickknacks I'm not going to sell. They've been promised to other family members. Where should I put them so they're out of your way," I asked Sarah who already wrapped three of the crystal goblets in newspaper.

"I wanna see!" Tina squealed. "There is so much neat stuff here, I wanna see what you're keeping. I wanna see!"

Sarah looked around. "How about on the dresser? We're not taking the bedroom set and we'll know not to touch anything there."

She gently took my hand and led me into the bathroom, out of earshot of Tina.

"My daughter was in a car accident and has some brain damage. She doesn't mean any harm. But she talks a lot," she told me.

"Not to worry. I can use some conversation to get my mind off what's going on." I squeezed her hand to let Sarah know I welcomed their company.

She smiled and went back to work. While we'd been talking, Roger had loaded up four chairs and the dinette table on a wheeled dolly and pushed them toward the elevator. While each empty space created lightened the weight I felt on my chest a tiny little bit, it was soon replaced with much sorrow. There would be no more laughter around the dining room table while blowing out birthday candles on pretty store bought cakes, no more ice cubes from trays because the ice maker didn't work and no more rides in the elevator to June's fifth floor apartment. The rituals binding our friendship together no longer existed.

I lined up post office 'if it fits it ships' boxes in the bedroom, one for each of the recipients on June's list. As I came across the named items, I set them in the appropriate box and checked it off. I meant to sort through the linen closet and today seemed like a good day for that. As usual I got sidetracked into another room, which needed just as much of my attention as the rest of the home.

In the corner of the guest bedroom, was a small dresser with a four-shelf bookcase on top. The piece had originally been in my bedroom in Cleveland as a teenager. Somewhere along the line, Mom sent it to me and when Richard and I didn't have room for it any longer in our home, I gave it to Dad and June. The shelves were filled with old books.

Roger decided he liked it and could sell it for a good price. He asked me to empty the bookshelves so he could move it. June and I never liked to read the same kinds of books. She was into mass-market paperbacks of mysteries or spy thrillers. Me, I preferred stories about the human condition and the struggles of life with pretty covers and blurbs by well-known authors.

On these shelves I found a collection of thick, old, worn novels with stiff black bindings and faded gold lettered titles.

Look Homeward Angel by Thomas Wolfe.

I flipped open the front cover. Inside, old newspaper articles about Thomas Wolfe, the author, were pasted. A story about his return to Lancaster, Pennsylvania to connect with the other branch of the Wolfe family had several entries underlined in pen.

June often told me Thomas Wolfe was her cousin. I did a little research on him and the dates didn't seem to match up. I ignored the notion she could actually be related to a famous writer as another of her airs of pretentiousness. It made her feel important to rattle on about him so I let her. He was born in 1900 and she, not until 1921. Maybe I'd find the connection she insisted existed and I never quite believed, inside these family treasured volumes. I leafed through a few more of the books. Old and yellowed newspaper clippings fell to the floor.

I read *Look Homeward Angel* at her insistence and absolutely loved it. Thomas Wolfe was a story telling genius but unfortunately his life was cut short in his thirties by tuberculosis in his brain. His novels are considered classics but are not nearly as well known as Hemingway or Fitzgerald.

"Are you done in there Miss Linda?" Roger called out. "I'm ready to take the dresser."

"Not quite," I answered, gathering up a stack of the books to carrying them to my special place in the other room. I wanted to sit and look through the books alone and unbothered by the commotion going on all around me, but Roger had a truck to load.

I dumped out the contents of three drawers onto the guest bed and cleared the bookcase of the rest of its books. For the first time since I arrived here, I felt excited about something. I would have a lot of reading to do. Books could do that to me, any kind of book, old, new or something in between. These books sparked a bond, something I'd been searching for, for a long time.

It surprised me she hadn't left these books to someone on her list. I suspect June knew me well enough to know I'd take them no matter what she wrote on the dreaded list. The books themselves had broken bindings and lots of handwritten notes in the margins so were probably not worth much in their current condition, but the family history contained on the pages was priceless. I was not a Wolfe, but I had a connection with June that made us feel like family even if her blood didn't run through my veins.

I had quite a collection of old books, more than twenty volumes by or about Thomas Wolfe stacked in the corner by the time I moved them all. I caressed the old faded covers hoping some of the author's brilliance would enlighten my creative muse. More importantly I wanted to curl up on the sofa that Roger declined to take, and start reading. Engrossing myself in a Thomas Wolfe novel was sure to stop the world racing around me. I wanted to read, learn and enjoy all that his talent could impart on me, a working author striving to become the caliber of a best selling writer. On some level I was a student of literature of all kinds. I decided right then, they were going home with me.

Each time I passed the linen closet on the way to hide my stash of books, it called my name.

"I know. I hear you," I said.

The diversion of the bookcase over, it was time to start on the linen closet. It was small and wouldn't be such an overwhelming task to me while still on my antique book high. The folding metal door screeched when I pulled on the handle.

"Oh, that sent shivers up my spine!" Tina yelled out.

I yanked at it again before it loosened up and allowed me to see what had been hidden behind closed doors. Frayed edge towels and sheets stuffed the wire shelves exactly what should be stored in a linen closet.

"Sarah, do you want any towels?" I shouted over the sound of pots and pans clattering.

"We always need extra towels for cushions," Tina answered for her.

It appeared to me Tina had all the answers. She sat on the sofa, in June's worn and faded spot, supervising the proceedings, laughing and giggling every time her mother shouted, "Look at this! Do you want us to take this?"

I stopped what I was doing to see what she had.

Sarah placed a large wooden silver chest, I never saw before on the kitchen counter. I flipped up the lid. Wrapped in faded blue anti tarnish cloths was a sterling silver service for twelve, of knives, forks, spoons and every kind serving piece imaginable from a dressing spoon to a fish server to set of long handled ice tea spoons. Having researched sterling silver flatware sets belonging to my mother and Richard's mother, I knew this was another one of those things whose value would not match its beauty. As we age, things we hold dear lose value, just as our minds deteriorate holding onto wisdoms a younger generation will never understand.

I thought about her question for a minute, "You can take it."

Sarah inventoried the pieces and wrote it down on her list.

I went back to the closet, hoping I could get at least one task completely finished today in the hubbub of activity that surrounded me instead of half of many. Pulling out a stack of poorly folded, worn and frayed sheets, a book fell out landing on the floor with a thud.

Startled, Tina cried out, "What was that?"

"Just a photo album." I opened it up to see a picture of Steve's daughters, Alex and Lauren as little girls all dressed up in frilly dresses, sitting on a bench with their cousin, Luke. Luke is close to twenty years older than the girls. He's tall and lanky and looked like a giant next to the children. My heart warmed at the sweetness of the photo.

I flipped through a few more pages of family snapshots, remembering us all at different phases of our lives. We were skinny, had big hair and wore some really ugly and outlandish clothes. The kids were little, cute and always smiling in the photos. Memories turned the clock backwards, a welcome relief in the middle of the day. When I was ready to close the book, I turned the pages back to their original position. And then I noticed it. In the upper left hand corner of the inside cover, a name, In June's handwriting. "Steve".

I pushed open the folding door a bit further for a better view inside. Seven more photo albums of varying colors, blue, green, burgundy, all the same size with the word "Photos" embossed in gold on the front cover. I opened each album after pulling them from their hiding place. Inside each front cover, a name, one for me, each of my sisters and brother. The remaining four contained the names of June's niece and three nephews.

All those pictures sent in a birthday card or Christmas card to an old woman to show her how cute and smart, educated and well traveled we all were, had been saved. This was our way of making sure she could see our children grow up since she lived so far away. I had often wondered how June spent her days, and neatly filing away summer vacation pictures of her stepchildren had never crossed my mind as being one of her activities.

"Ooo. Can I see?" yelped Tina. "I love looking at pictures."

"Tina, don't you go bothering Miss Linda. She's got work to do too," Sarah chimed in clutching a plate and a newspaper in her hands.

"It's okay. I don't mind." I handed one of the albums to Tina. She eagerly opened it and examined each photo closely as if she personally knew the people in the pictures.

I set the other albums next to their respective boxes and went back to trying to empty the closet. A spot of color on the top shelf caught my eye as a welcome change to the dull white linens on the lower shelves.

On my tiptoes, I reached to pull down a patchwork quilt. It landed in my arms. I unfolded the coverlet, releasing a musty odor of years of being hidden in darkness. I didn't find the pattern particularly attractive, but I admit knowing nothing about quilting. June spoke of these quilts, watching her mother hand stitch them when she was a child, but I'd never seen them. Varying sizes of pink and white triangles were framed by large solid squares of a mustard yellow with black flecks like pepper and trimmed in a darker shade pink. Maybe it was a less faded version of the same hue.

"Can I see the quilt?" Tina had snuck up behind me and peered over my shoulder. "I love quilts. Momma, we can sell this one easy."

"Tina. What did I ask you to do?" Sarah made her way from the kitchen to see the new treasure. She fingered the edge between her thumb and forefinger. "This is on old one, handmade."

"I know. June's mother made it." I looked into their faces, wide eyed and tentative awaiting my answer. "I'm going to take these to June. They might help to make her feel more at home."

The crowd around me dissipated.

Another quilt remained wedged on the top shelf. I reached up to get it down. It felt much heavier than the one that reminded me of the food at a baseball game with its color of hot dogs and mustard with all the trimmings. On a white background, lay a multi colored pattern of hexagon shaped pieces. Larger than the first, I carried it to the bed to unfold it. As I did, a surprise revealed itself. A flimsy shirt sized white box, the kind they used to give away years ago at the department store as a gift box. I spotted it, 'Linda', written on the top in the corner.

Could it be? The box of personal papers June wrote in her letter to the lawyer? I stared at it; afraid to even touch it, not knowing what family secret might be lurking inside. She wanted her possessions of value to go to my siblings, her niece, nephews and goddaughter. I was the one who drove her to the store, took her out to dinner and the movies, while the others all lived a thousand miles away in different directions. There has to be something in the box, she feels is far more valuable than anything else she owns.

Bantering between Sarah and her daughter interrupted my thoughts.

"I like this basket, Mama. Can I have it?" asked Tina.

"You know we don't take anything. Ask Miss Linda if we can buy it," responded Sarah.

Through all the mother daughter chatter, Roger never spoke. He worked methodically, hoisting heavy furniture onto the dolly, rolling it down the Chattahoochee covered hallway clicking and clacking as he went. Most of the larger pieces had disappeared leaving the marks of crushed carpeting where they'd once rested. The apartment slowly began to release itself of its possessions.

The basket in question sat at Tina's feet. I had no special attachment to it but instead of offering it to them right off, I waited for one of them to speak.

"Can we buy the basket from you?" Sarah asked.

"I don't want it. You can have it," I said.

"No, we don't take anything. We run an honest business." She tucked a ten-dollar bill in my palm.

"Sarah, it's really not necessary," I said.

"For us it is," she answered.

Working side by side with this family all morning, little by little, I relaxed. They were kind and genuine in their own folksy way. I began to let my guard down and the fear of Roger driving off with June's things never to be seen again had dissipated. Now that Sarah had shown me honesty that came from deep in her heart, I felt safe and comforted. I'd made a good choice in helping June.

I slipped the bill in my pocket. Tina grinned from ear to ear without saying a word.

The box lay on the bed, still and silent, exerting some kind of wild energy keeping me away from it. I picked up the corners of the quilt and slid the mystery box onto the bed without touching it.

"The difference between a mountain and a molehill is your perspective."

CHAPTER THIRTEEN

Dad and June moved to the east coast by the time our next summer visit rolled around. They lived in an apartment on East 59th Street and Sutton Place, a long block from the East River, in New York City on the 16th floor. With a view of the city, at night we watched the lights come on in the Empire State Building and the top of the Chrysler Building from the tiled terrace that ran the length of the apartment. The living room was big, bright and roomy with wood floors and windows on two sides.

New York City, with its never-ending noisy car horns and loud fire engine sirens, was a far cry from the green suburbs of Cleveland. Steve and I got used to apartment living in Seattle with swimming pools and fitness rooms, but here the buildings were crowded together in a jungle made of concrete. This summer would be different than the others.

June's furniture looked different in the city. Some new pieces had been added to the odd assortment of contemporary pieces mixed with antiques. A glass coffee table sat on a heavy gold-flecked curly cue base. A ceramic tulip and a Royal Dalton Toby mug decorated the top along with the latest *Women's Wear Daily* Dad hadn't read yet. My mother had Royal Dalton figurines so I knew what they were, and I wanted badly to pick up the tulip and examine it, but was afraid. These were all still June's things and I still wasn't certain if I could touch them without being told no.

Down the hall were two bedrooms and two bathrooms. Dad and June's room was large and Steve and I slept in what they called the den. This is the room we watched TV in at night. Dad had a chair, his and his alone and June shared the red pull out sofa with us when we were visiting. When it was time for bed, we pushed the other furniture to the side and pulled out the mattress. Steve and I would dive in from the foot since mere inches were left on either side of the room. We lifted Maggie and Molly, the poodles, onto the bed for our goodnight kisses.

The big city amazed Steve and me, being kids from the suburbs. The steamy asphalt streets packed with cars and the sizzling concrete sidewalks crowded with people moving at a frantic pace. I never heard so many horns honking at the same time. People walked their dogs letting them poop on the sidewalk. It took me most of the summer to learn to vigilantly watch every step I took when out in the concrete maze.

During the day on the terrace, where we hung out in between trips to the grocery store for more Dr. Pepper and big bags of potato chips, both things Mom never allowed us, June showed us where the celebrities in the neighborhood lived.

"Hermione Gingold lives in that building," she pointed out.

I had no idea who Hermione Gingold might be but June thought she was famous and worth noting.

"Oh, really," I responded.

"And over there, is David Brinkley's apartment. See the window with the lamp," she said.

I knew David Brinkley and his partner, Chet Huntley. At the time, in 1969, every television set in America tuned them in for their evening newscast.

"Hopefully tonight we'll run into Gordon McRae when we go out for dinner. I think your father wants to take you to the Mayfair. If Gordon comes in for a drink, he'll sit at the piano and sing," June told us.

Once again I wasn't quite sure who Gordon McRae was but I did know Meredith McRae from Petticoat Junction fame, one of my favorite TV shows. I figured they must be related so I felt excited about seeing a celebrity in person.

June became animated when talking about the sightings of famous people she'd heard about from the cashier in the grocery store or her hairdresser on the corner. I didn't recognize the names of most of the ones she talked about, but I listened carefully just in case she heard something about The Beatles appearing on Ed Sullivan show and I could bug Dad for tickets since we were in New York.

The Mayfair was located on First Avenue and 53rd Street, and it was Dad's favorite place. Dinner out meant I changed into a dress and combed my hair. Steve put on pants and a collared shirt. No shorts allowed. June also put on a dress, high heels and a string of pearls.

As typical kids, Steve and I raced down the hall to see who could hit the elevator call button first. He usually won. He had longer legs. Dad walked behind us, laughing at our antics, while June locked the apartment door.

The Mayfair was a dark restaurant and bar with rich walnut paneling on the walls, black leather upholstery on the booths and chairs, dimly lit with reproduction gaslights on the wall. Hardly a place for impressionable young teenagers, but it's the kind of place Dad loved to enjoy his martini while June smoked her cigarettes after a long day of putting up with us.

We ordered dinner before the keys on the piano began to tinkle. Words to a song glided through the air.

"It's Gordon McRae," June squealed.

If it hadn't been in the days long before smart phones and selfies, June would have taken a picture of him. She positively glowed. She lifted her drink in the direction of the piano when he finished. He lifted his back. Dad grinned happy to see his Junie having a good time. Steve and I half-heartedly applauded to be polite. The music was definitely not the Rolling Stones.

Gordon McRae launched into *The Surry with the Fringe on Top*. I knew the words this time so I sang along in between bites of a perfectly cooked T-bone steak and a baked potato loaded with bacon, cheddar cheese and butter.

To this day I have a pretty broad repertoire of Broadway songs in my head. Susan loved to play the piano and sing. Her sheet music consisted of the latest and most popular hits such as *The Music Man*, *Oliver*, *West Side Story* and *My Fair Lady*. Whenever she wanted to play, she called for the chorus. We never dreamed of refusing since she was the oldest after all. She played and Martha and I would belt out the tunes. Actually Susan would belt them out and drown us out. She had an *Oklahoma* song book too, because the words came easily to me as June's heart throb performed the title song for the bar patrons.

Nothing much made my brother happy at anytime, at least not that I could see. He effortlessly blended into the wood paneling at The Mayfair. Although we always went to my father's for the summer together, I have very little recollection of him saying anything, being anywhere or even giving a damn about Gordon McRae and his rendition of *Oklahoma*. That's how our summer visitations unfolded every year until we were too old to go. Dad went along with whatever June got excited about. I wanted to try every new pizza place or ice cream parlor she read about in the New York Times, and Steve tagged along never voicing an opinion.

Women surrounded Steve, being the only boy. Dad came from a small town in Michigan and lost his mother at an early age. He got to college by being an athlete and expected his own son to have the same physical abilities. All four of us however, inherited my mother's klutziness when it came to sports. These were the sixties and although the girls were expected to go to college, I don't think my parents had any high hopes of big careers from any of us. Those demands however were different for the only boy. I suspected Dad wanted something more out of Steve because he was the only son. That Steve didn't have what Dad wanted may have been the reason for his apparent apathy.

* * *

Now having been exposed to the celebrity New York City had to offer, I was soon exposed to something dirtier and more sinister about living in a big city. Our bellies full and show tunes dancing in our heads, we headed straight to the den and the comfort of the red sofa. Dad settled in to his chair and turned on *Hawaii 5-0*. I curled up in the corner of the sofa closest to him. He reached over and rubbed the top of my foot that hung over the arm of the couch.

"Linda, go wash your feet. They're filthy," he said.

"Huh?" I gave a typical thirteen-year-old answer before twisting my right foot around to see what he was talking about. "Ooo. Gross. Where did that come from?"

At home in Cleveland, I went barefoot all summer and my feet never ended up looking like this, pitch black from toe to heel. Following Dad's instructions, I sat on the edge of the tub and scrubbed my feet. Rivers of black sooty water curled down the drain. When my feet were sufficiently clean, I dried them off and padded back down the hallway to my place on the red sofa.

"Linny," my father said this time in a happier tone of voice. Linny was my nickname. We each had one. Susie Booze, Marthy, Steve Boy and Linny. And we knew the difference between being called our pet name or our full given name. "You can't go barefoot while outside on the patio. Put some shoes on."

"How come?" I'd never been a child to take instruction well. With a curious mind, I asked a laundry list of questions until I fully grasped the purpose of the action.

"This is the city. It's dirty. You track soot all over the house and Junie has to clean it." He had taken his eyes from the television and stared directly into mine. "Understand?"

"OK."

* * *

The next day the lesson of dirt versus cleanliness would be solidly driven into my head. How dirty and disgusting New York City could be was about to teach me the true meaning of last night's lecture. Dad ate his daily breakfast of Special K with skim milk that gave the golden flakes a grayish tinge, popped his dose of vitamin C, put on his suit coat and walked out the door to work. That was the cue for Steve and me to make the bed and put the red sofa back to its normal sitting position.

At home we were required to wash our own dishes, or at least get them into the dishwasher. June never accepted our offers to help. She didn't want us under foot. She was used to cleaning up by herself because she'd been single, living alone for most of her life. Possibly it was because the kitchen in this apartment was the smallest on the planet. One person barely had room to turn around in it.

A tiny galley kitchen was tucked into the corner of the dining room. A swinging door hid it from the view from the living room. The door could only be opened enough to squeeze through without hitting the garbage can along the wall in front of the refrigerator. Counters lined each side with a sink and dishwasher on one and the stove and oven on the other. The kitchen had a window looking out on the terrace, so at least you had light to see if you were about to bump into the misplaced handle of a hot pan.

While June finished cleaning up the breakfast dishes, Steve watched game shows and I wrote letters. Yesterday June took me to a huge Hallmark store on Fifth Avenue and I bought three new boxes of stationary. I studied each box carefully before selecting the red, white and blue paper for today's correspondence. Writing letters was my lifeline to my usual teenage life back home. I wrote page after page to my best friend, Georgia, about the big city lights, buying a delicious hot dog from a corner vendor, and our trip to the Museum of Modern Art. June gave me a stamp and I rushed out to the hallway to drop it in the mail slot by the elevator.

The rest of the morning was spent riding up and down the elevator to the dank and dreary basement of the building with the laundry. I got the creeps every time I went down there, past the rows of storage lockers with metal grates for walls. Inside I could see the piles of over stuffed and misshapen cardboard boxes, discarded end tables and the now shade-less lamps that once sat on top of them. The old musty smell of cold and dampness changed slightly when I got to the laundry room to include a hint of bleach. Several well used washers and dryers all sporting a locked box attached to the top with a metal slide. Laundry here required quarters another new concept for the girl from the suburbs.

I helped June carry the dirty sheets and clothes. She threw her coin purse on top of the basket and we made our way into the depths of the earth underneath the floors of urban dwellers. Dad had a habit of emptying the change from his pockets each night when he came home from work. I suspect June picked out all the quarters when he wasn't looking and stashed them in her little black coin purse. During the week, the laundry room wasn't busy so we were able to find empty washers for all of our loads.

"I hate it down here," June said. "It gives me the creepy crawlies." She scratched her forearm before reaching for her head.

"It smells kinda gross," I added. At home I did my own laundry so it was kind of nice to have company to talk to while navigating the cold, dark city basement. June and I never seemed to run out of stupid teenager things to discuss. I think she read my *Seventeen* magazines when I wasn't looking. She loved fashion and makeup at any level.

Just then I heard a loud snap. I looked at June and she at me. We didn't want to know what it was but I suspected a rat had just met his demise. It could have been some pipes rattling. I tried my best to believe it was the latter. The basement wasn't ever a quiet place, with a symphony of strange beeps, bumps and clacks. We hurried back upstairs to wait for the loads to finish.

June sent Steve and me back to the basement armed with her coin purse when it was time to put the loads in the dryer. Steve didn't appear to be bothered by any of it. June said boys were no good at folding so I accompanied her when the clothes were dry. We didn't waste time talking however, and got right to the task at hand. My skin crawled as a cockroach ran in front of my feet. I didn't dare scream. June was now scratching her arms and head at more frequent intervals.

The morning had been taken up with laundry and the afternoon would be filled with the art of grocery shopping in the crowded city. I always enjoyed food shopping with Mom at Heinen's, our neighborhood supermarket where they put a number on your cart when you checked out. You dropped the full cart off at the special pick up room and then drove your car up to the door so the contents could be loaded into the trunk without you lifting a finger. The protocol in New York City for buying and getting the food safely to home and into the kitchen cupboard was a very different experience.

The aisles at D'Agastino's were narrow, barley enough room for one person to walk single file. And they were tall. If June, at barely five foot two, needed something off the top shelf, she was out of luck. Maybe the store had an employee in charge of helping customers in that situation who carried a reacher stick, the kind with a rubber claw at the end, but I never saw one.

The three of us squeezed through the aisles, collecting the items June instructed us to get into the miniature sized shopping cart.

"Go get the kind of pop you want to drink," she said.

Steve and I rushed to the drink section.

"Orange Crush," Steve demanded.

"Dr. Pepper," I whined.

We hogged the aisle arguing over which six pack to purchase knowing we wouldn't be able to carry more than one home with all the other food already in the cart. June came around the corner.

"We can get both. I'm having our order delivered,'" she said. "We'll take the ice cream though so it doesn't melt."

My brother and I looked at each other with wide eyes.

Delivered? This was 1969. We never heard of grocery delivery. Was it that June was buying ice cream? Dad loved ice cream, especially Dairy Queen.

In New York City however, there wasn't a Dairy Queen so almost every evening, after dinner, the four of us walked down the street to Baskin Robbins and got whichever one of the thirty one flavors that struck our fancy that day. I rarely strayed from my usual favorite mint chocolate chip. Having ice cream at home would be a break in the routine.

"It's a surprise," June told us.

We were all in for a surprise as long as it involved eating ice cream, and having some leftovers handy in the freezer for seconds.

A knock on the door announced the grocery delivery about an hour later. I helped June put them away. Everything came packed in brown paper bags that we lined up on the kitchen counter until there was no more room, the rest went on the floor. That left little space for the two of us to navigate. I put the bananas on the counter and a swarm of tiny flying bugs came with them. I haphazardly slapped the air to put an end to the swarm.

"Linda," June screamed. "What's in my hair?"

She bent her head down in my direction. I understood by this action, I was supposed to look for something moving in the nest of golden, tease and sprayed hair.

"I don't see anything," I said glancing slightly without touching the highly teased hotbed.

"There's a bug in my hair," she squealed while hopping up and down. "Go get my hairbrush. It's in the bathroom. Hurry!"

I walked down the hall at my usual pace. There wasn't a bug in her hair. At least I didn't see one. June's voice climbed a couple octaves whenever she got excited and it seemed to me she did that a lot, over one of her unknown celebrities, creepy noises in the basement laundry and now a bug. At thirteen, I didn't yet grasp the different levels of urgency in my own mother's life let alone those of my stepmother.

I'd never been invited into the master bedroom; I only ever viewed it from the doorway. The bathroom oozed of the same sweet and soapy fragrance that accompanied Dad and June wherever they lived. The older I got, the more sickening the odor became to me, the comfort of sitting on the bathroom floor watching my father shave turned into a distant memory. A hard brush, with loads of brown wiry hair wrapped around the bristles perched on the edge of the sink. I picked it up.

With the windows open to let in what little breeze existed, June's screams could be heard over the constant cacophony of honking horns and ambulance sirens. In Cleveland, a neighbor would soon be knocking on the door to make sure no one inside was being murdered. Here, if anyone were home, they'd just turn up the volume on the television and return to the intensity of today's soap opera storyline and wait to see what happened next door on the evening news.

"Hurry! Linda, hurry!" Her muffled screaming sounded more desperate even with the long hallway between us. Not understanding why anyone would get so excited over a little bug, I saw no urgency in the situation. I pushed open the kitchen door a few inches as far as it would go and squeezed the brush into June's wriggling grip.

Brush in hand; June kneeled on the kitchen floor among the brown paper bags. With hard, furious strokes, she tried to brush the bug off her head.

"Ooo, Ooo," she shrieked. I never heard such a sound out of a human being before. High and squeaky, half bird like, half like an oink of a pig. I stood motionless, Steve lay sprawled out on the couch reading his Mad Magazine.

"It's crawling on my head! Where is it?" She brushed more furiously. "Ow. Ow. Ooo."

I thought she brushed all the hair right off her head when June's bright red face looked up at me. With tears running down her cheeks she announced, "I think I got it." She brushed a couple more final strokes before crawling away from the door. I came in and helped her get up off her knees, while scouring the room with my eyes for the escaping bug.

As an observer, I never saw any kind of bug fall from her head and scurry under the refrigerator and I think she lost half a head of her colored and permed hair that day. The bug episode became my first exposure to the highly excitable, tense and mercurial June. Next to my reserved and often apathetic view of the world, I wondered if we would ever get along with one another. She was so different from my own mother who I felt very little for, and at this age I still struggled with knowing how she fit into the puzzle of my life. Would my stepmother fall into a similar kind of distant and uncaring parental relationship with me and the rest of her stepchildren?

I remember the date of the real or maybe imaginary bug well. July 20, 1969, the day Neil Armstrong walked on the moon. When we watched it on television. Dad, Steve and I took our usual places in the den and glued our eyes to the screen as he spoke those famous words, "One small step for man. One giant leap for mankind."

"Wow, how do they send the TV picture all the way from the moon?" I asked.

I grew up watching rocket launches on television. In elementary school, the teachers would pack us into the music room; bring in a small black and white television propped up on a wheeled cart. In unison all the kids would countdown ten, nine, eight until we arrived at one and the space capsule lifted off over a ball of smoke and fire. Man now walked on the moon, which meant our world was changing and growing at a mind blowing pace.

With our minds engaged with what was happening over two hundred thousand miles away on the surface of the moon, June appeared in the doorway.

"How about some dessert?" she smiled without a trace of the bug episode in her voice. "It's moon cake."

Handing us each a plate, I spotted a heaping scoop of vanilla ice cream between two fat gooey chocolate brownies. Being so excited over the ice cream, I never noticed the brownies amongst the groceries. I ate my moon cake in honor of the first man on the moon and wondered if June ever told my father about the bug.

If she did tell him I can hear the conversation in my head.

"Junie. It's just a bug. It's wouldn't hurt you."

"But it was crawling on my head!" she'd say.

"Oh. You're imagining things," he'd answer.

I am my father's daughter after all.

"The worst bullies you will ever encounter in your life, are your own thoughts."
— Bryant McGill

CHAPTER FOURTEEN

By early afternoon, the kitchen cupboards were empty and the dining room stacked with boxes. The table and chairs I used as my desk had disappeared. Only the upholstered sofa and side chairs remained. Roger told me right off the bat he wasn't interested in those. The bareness of the place should have brought relief, but it didn't.

A good stiff drink probably wouldn't calm my frazzled nerves either. June still had a bottle of Robert Mondavi chardonnay in the refrigerator waiting for me. When I stopped drinking in 2010 she kept a bottle on hand just in case I ever changed my mind if I came to visit. She never thought she had a drinking problem even though she couldn't go a day without one. Therefore I didn't have a drinking problem either. That's how June saw just about everything in life. If it didn't affect her, it didn't affect anyone else she knew either. I thought about the chilled bottle waiting patiently for me and only me every moment of the day.

"Miss Linda, we don't want all the canned goods in here," Sarah stuck her head in the pantry and held up a can of Progresso. "But there's some vodka in here. Five big bottles. We can sell that."

"You can sell the vodka?" I didn't believe her. Who would buy open bottles of vodka at a furniture auction?

June loved her vodka almost as much as she loved her cigarettes. Every night before dinner, she eyeballed and poured what she called a half a shot into an old fashioned glass over some ice and then added water. She convinced herself she restricted her alcohol consumption in roughly the same manner she did cigarettes. Only for a drink, she never measured anything and had no tally sheet and tiny yellow pencil to help her keep track. After dinner, the glass was refilled more than once with mostly water according to the drunken old woman. If she'd marked her vodka bottles like she did her cigarettes, June might have to admit she drank more than her share.

The yellow pages became June's best friend after Richard and I moved away and our outings ceased to exist. She scoured those pages under "L" for liquor stores until she found one to deliver a case of half gallons of the cheapest vodka on the shelves. The delivery charge most likely added up to more than the cost of the rotgut liquor. Even on her limited income, her priorities became fixed and non-negotiable. Cigarettes, then vodka followed by a few groceries and the electric bill.

"You'd be surprised at what some people will buy. We'll sell this as a lot, all five bottles together," Sarah said.

"Help yourself," I said. "Can you sell cigarettes? I'm sure there are some Virginia Slims hidden around here somewhere."

"Not allowed to sell cigarettes. But if we could, there'd be a buyer."

"It does smell kind of smoky in here," Tina piped in.

My plug in air fresheners weren't doing their job. My throat dry and scratchy, my temples throbbed as usual.

When the Tennessee family had taken all they could fit in their truck, I signed the inventory sheet and hugged them each goodbye. In their own funny, homespun way, they made this day bearable. They packed up with lightening speed and I could finally see some progress.

As always I had one more job before my day could be finished, I went to visit June. Seeing her, confused and helpless, made me sad. But it also served to keep me focused on my task, to take care of Junie. Without her, I wouldn't have a purpose in my life right now. I'd be at home pretending to write the next great American novel while I purposely distracted myself with email and Facebook accomplishing nothing. We developed a symbiotic relationship that brought us to this point.

I folded up the quilts and put the box on top of them. Hopefully I'd gather up the guts to look inside once I got to my hotel for the night.

At Hawthorne, I found June in her usual position, curled up in bed.

"June, look what I brought you," I said holding up the hot dog quilt.

She sat up and stared at me. "You know you really don't have to send all my things to everybody. It's kind of silly to do it, you know."

Now she tells me.

I've anguished over making sure I did what she wanted. I made her cantankerous, for her own well being, and miserable by forcing her to move where she could get daily assistance she was convinced she didn't need. My entire day was consumed with decisions about her possessions, what should go, what should stay and how to get rid of what was left. In some small way, I thought by doing that for her, I could ease her pain. I was actually trying to create some kind of calm out of chaos for myself.

"Didn't your mother make these quilts?" I asked.

"Every stitch." June slowly ran her weathered and frail hands over the fabric.

"Do you want one on your bed?" I asked.

"That would be nice. I miss my mother. The white one," she said.

I spread the prettier of the quilts over her and folded it back so only her feet were underneath it. Her body relaxed.

Who is this woman with the drooping skin and weary eyes? Who is she who finds such comfort from the thought of a mother I had never met? Who is she to me and why am I here right now with her? She's not my mother. I had a mother with whom I had nothing in common. June did not give me her blood yet I am the one here doing my best to make sure she is comfortable and cared for. No one is waiting in the wings to give either of us a few minutes of peace from the constant struggle between the two of us.

My mother, Sallie, wasn't mean or evil in any way. She went to church every Sunday, but was lost and depressed most of her life, getting married during World War II when my father came home on leave and having children she didn't really want because that was expected of her. As mother and daughter we wrestled, rarely finding any common ground, similar to what June and I are experiencing at this moment in time.

Mom died in 2001, a week after her eightieth birthday. She'd been ill and in a nursing home for more than five years. I had nothing that belonged to her nor did I long for anything of hers. My siblings and I emptied out her New York City rent controlled apartment one hot summer. The situation was much like this one. Mom was still alive and living in a nursing home where she would remain for the rest of her life.

I reflected on the similarity that had suddenly come to mind. Yet in Mom's case my sisters and brother came together, although not willingly, to pack up and dispose her possessions. Susan came equipped with rubber gloves and a mask so not to intake any of my mother's germs while she rifled through Mom's books and old papers. Steve brought Karen with him, the only one of us who felt he needed to drag a spouse through the perils of my mother's life. My recollection is the two of them sat on the sofa holding hands, while the rest of us attempted to cut through the layers of New York City grime. Sallie, even on a good day, was not a good housekeeper. Martha and I always took a taxi by ourselves and it wasn't the first time the siblings found themselves on opposite sides of the family equation, split in two.

Later in her life, my mother told me her children didn't care about her, never realizing she'd never given them any reason to. I believe that explains the emotional detachment from my family I've experienced most of my life. We were all looking for love within our home but we were unwilling to give to each other. I didn't grow up in a close or loving family. My sisters had gone off to college by the time my parents divorced. Steve, he's a boy and he's just Steve. I grew up in a world I created for myself, separate from my sisters and brother. The older we got the deeper the chasm became.

This time, however, I was the one left to handle the family drama on my own. Did they think blood is thicker than water? They felt obligated to do it for Mom but left June to fend for herself. Blood isn't the only thing that defines a family or an obligation. Why am I the only one of us who knew that? Because they hadn't heard my father's voice over and over in their heads for the past 25 years. I was the only one there to help him die, and he and June were a package deal. My job was to help her die too, so they could be together once again.

I'm not Cinderella and June is not the wicked stepmother trying to find the right fit for the glass slipper. On his deathbed, Dad asked me to take care of her. He didn't ask me to care for my own mother, my sisters or my brother. Or even his dog, Shana, who he adored. He didn't ask me to take care of myself. He said Junie. I've never forgotten those final words. Dad never said goodbye to me, maybe this was my chance to hear it from him.

Dad found love that transcended all others with June, and she with him. His children did not sit in first place in his life, June did. I still hadn't come to terms with that all these years later, because we didn't have priority in Mom's life either. A child begins searching for the ultimate confirmation of love from the moment of birth. I never had a chance of finding it and my selfish side wanted Dad's final send off to belong to me and not anyone else.

"Where did you find my mother's quilts?" June asked.

Afraid of the response my truthful answer might invoke, "They were in your closet here on the shelf," I said settling for a half-truth.

June's face softened when she held her mother's quilt, a calm, peaceful state not seen in a very long time. She spoke occasionally of Mother and Daddy but I didn't know much about them. On the wall in June's guest room hung a collage of old faded photographs, one of which was her mother and father standing in front of an empty, wire, grocery store shopping cart. I found the picture odd. Taken long before the age of smart phones and instant photo opportunities, someone had an actual camera handy in a supermarket parking lot, shot the picture and had the film developed. Then the print found it's way into an envelope with a short note to a daughter far away. Every picture sent to her over the years, was sorted and lovingly placed in a personalized photo album or in a frame to be hung on the wall. I learned of June's special hobby preserving cherished keepsakes only today.

"I'm glad you brought them," she said. "I'm so cold here. The quilt will keep me warm. I wonder why no one got them out of the closet for me."

"That's where the pink one is if you need it. I'll tell the aide when she comes so she knows if you want it," I said.

"You would do that for me?" June asked.

"Of course I would." I squeezed her tiny hand.

June's eyes twinkled while gazing at the quilts that had long been tucked away in the closet. They must have sparked some childhood memory of watching her mother sew them in a room filled with fabric, needles and thread she could no longer articulate. At this moment I wanted to feel the same kind of maternal love that June felt. I had to dig deep to find a similar kind of handmade love in my own life.

Being the youngest, I never witnessed my mother sewing or making crafts but I do have one item, and each of my siblings has a similar one. A handmade Christmas stocking with our name embroidered across the top. Mine is green felt cut with pinking shears, with bells hand sewn across the top just under my name. My stocking has a brown teddy bear with blue sequins for eyes and a nose; a pink felt Tinkerbelle and a charm of ballet slippers. Each holiday when I find it in the box of decorations, I tell whoever is nearby, "My Mom made this for me". Every Christmas to this day Santa stuffs it with gifts. This is the single memory of my mother I cling to.

* * *

I spent three more days cleaning and sorting what was left in the apartment, signing a contract with a realtor and making arrangements to have the place painted and the carpet cleaned. I couldn't wait to get home and get a kiss, first from Ginger and then from Richard. My eyes and throat needed a break from the constant onslaught of stale smoke. All this time the box remained in the trunk of my car, unopened. I packed as much as I could on top of it so I wouldn't be reminded it was waiting for me to look inside.

Since the box's discovery, when I arrived at the hotel at night, tired and sweaty, I conveniently forgot to bring the box inside. My daily visits with June left me more than afraid of the emotional turmoil I might face when I finally got up the courage to open it. I decided I wanted to be at home in my own comfortable surroundings before I took a peek at its contents.

I had one last chore to do before I could leave; send the boxes full of treasures to their intended recipients. That saddened me but I had to let go of my feelings so June could be at peace whether she was aware of it or not.

I found a paper written in June's scratchy writing of all of her contact information, buried in the piles of papers she left on her once neat and tidy desk. Amazingly enough there was an email address for Robin. I let Robin know what was happening and asked if she could verify her brother's addresses for me. The list looked old, Steve's address was one he'd moved out of a few years ago. I received a curt and succinct reply from her,

"I don't speak to my brothers and don't know where they live."

I thought my siblings were detached at the seams. We might not speak to each other very often but we know where each other lived and can find one another in an emergency. And we don't hold any animosity toward each other.

I learned as I grew older that families come in all levels of closeness, companionship and love. I still long to spend Thanksgiving around a large table with parents, grandparents, aunts, uncles, nieces, nephews and friends, filling every seat. A beautifully roasted turkey, cranberry sauce, stuffing and all the fixings grace the fancy tablecloth and are waiting to be devoured. The air is filled with laughter and a love of being together. That Norman Rockwell painting will never be mine. I wonder if Robin dreams of that too or if she's found a peace in what is not in her life either.

Off the tightly packed boxes went into the twilight zone each with a note handwritten from me inside.

I'm writing to let you know that June has moved to assisted living. She is suffering from dementia and is no longer able to care for herself. Her new address and phone are enclosed.

She's asked me to send these items to you and hopes you will cherish them as much as she did. If you have any questions, email me at this email address.

Linda

I specifically didn't give them my cell phone number not wanting to answer calls at all hours of the day and night. I've got enough of those to deal with. One of the nephews was supposedly off kilter but I didn't know why. I was unsure about the rest considering their sister didn't want to speak to them either. Email was far safer and much less intrusive in case one of them wanted something of June's not found in their box.

My last stop before I drove home was the one I had done each day since I'd arrived. Visit June. I dreaded it every time and today would be no different except for the fact that tomorrow it wouldn't be on my to do list. Every day I hoped I would find the June I used to know sitting in her chair, working a crossword puzzle, bright eyed and happy. I'm an optimist at heart and negative energy has its way of creeping into my psyche and wearing me down. I had hope for today; June would be more settled in her new home.

June lay in her usual position, curled up in bed lying on top of her mother's quilt wearing her new shoes, even though it was 10:30 in the morning. Her eyes closed, I tried not to disturb her before I could escape out the door unnoticed.

"Linda," June screeched. "What am I to do?"

"June, you don't have to do anything. Just relax. I've taken care of everything."

"I don't have to worry?" she asked.

"No. Enjoy yourself," I said.

"You would do that for me?" she whimpered.

"Of course I would," I answered.

"Okay," she said calmly.

I kissed her goodbye.

She wasn't the old June but she was a calmer June that day. I could safely leave her not knowing when I would return.

"No one saves us but ourselves. We ourselves must walk the path."
— Buddha

CHAPTER FIFTEEN

As Steve and I grew into teenagers with summer jobs, busy schedules and close friends to hang out with, our summer visits to see Dad and June didn't last for a full three weeks any longer. June still planned our excursions around the city to the Guggenheim Museum, an occasional Broadway show and to a pizza place she discovered in a magazine called Goldberg's Pizza. Dad loved that place, probably the real reason we ate there so often. He loved to comment how he didn't know how a Jewish man could make such good pizza.

Mom still drove us to the airport giving us instructions on how to behave as she drove. Dad picked us up and got us one of those big taxis with the fold up seats in back even though for the three of us we didn't need all that space. Steve and I thought those big taxis were cool.

When we arrived June was in the kitchen cooking the dreaded pot roast for dinner. Each time we came to New York, we had to get used to a new apartment. The days of the large wrap around terrace with views of the Empire State Building were gone. Each place seemed smaller and more cramped, barely enough room for four people even if we only stayed for a week.

Why they moved so much, I don't know. June was back working but Steve had started college. I wouldn't know until later that possibly Dad's gambling was the issue. He loved betting on the horses and he may have been losing more that he won. June went along with a smile on her face, claiming she wanted to live in a better building. I didn't stay long enough at this point to do laundry, so if these were buildings without bugs in the basement, I couldn't be certain.

In 1973 I went off to college at Bowling Green State University. It seemed like a good idea at the time since my parents told me I couldn't accept an offer from Wittenberg University, a private school in Springfield, Ohio. I was told there wasn't any money left to pay the pricey private school tuition. Susan and Steve had both gone to college there, Martha to similar sized school in Michigan. Didn't my parents realize they had four children who needed an education? I would get one; just one that was a lot cheaper.

I made the decision to major in Fashion Merchandising. When June started working as the dress buyer at Rogers Peet along side Dad, she sometimes took me with her to visit vendors on 6th Avenue in the fashion district when I was in town. I loved looking at all the new styles with her. I commented on the dresses I liked and didn't like and why. June wrote out her purchase orders for what she knew would sell.

We didn't agree but I learned that a smart clothing buyer didn't make selections based on their personal taste.

I never considered myself any kind of a fashionista even back then, but I did know what I didn't like. As the youngest child, I wore hand-me-downs. That might not be so bad except that my sisters were only 2 years apart and Mom dressed them alike. We have hundreds of photos of the two of them in the identical Christmas, Easter and back to school outfits. That meant I wore each one twice. First Martha's smaller size and then Susan's larger one. It made sense to me to break out into a style all my own.

The summer between my freshman and sophomore year of college, Mom sold the house in Cleveland and moved to New York City. Her job at McKinsey and Company in Cleveland had been transferred to the Big Apple. Mom insisted she wasn't searching for ways to get my father back; I secretly believed she was. I couldn't come up with any other reason for moving to New York. We were Midwesterners; Mom grew up in Detroit and had settled into a nice life in Cleveland with lots of friends, active in the church, a job she loved. I stayed in the same school district from first grade until high school graduation unlike my older sisters who changed schools every time Dad took a new job. She had roots here. Why upset the balance if she wasn't secretly searching for Dad?

I don't have a lot of memories of my parents together before they divorced. My father worked late nights and traveled quite a bit on buying trips. As kids we only remember one vacation that the six of us went on together. We lived in Minneapolis at the time, we were all packed in the car and Dad drove us to Mt. Rushmore and the Black

Hills. It's the one event in our childhood all four of us remember, even though each recollection is different. I was only four or five so Susan would have been twelve, Martha, ten and Steve, six.

My memories of Dad and June are as a couple. Everything about Mom is her as a single person. He had found the true love of his life, moved on and was never turning back. I never sensed even an ounce of discontent between my father and his Junie. Mom hadn't come to terms with living a single life, but she was not his college sweetheart any longer, that was clear to me.

Even though I had spent time in the city during summer vacations as a teenager visiting my father, being yanked out of my quiet suburban life was a shock to me. I felt lost and alone, without any friends or roots to ground me. I gained a built-in summer job at Rogers Peet, an old, established New England men's clothing store originally opened in 1874, since Dad was the president of the company. Once he showed me a custom suit he had hanging in his office, tailored for Bobby Kennedy shortly before his assassination. No one was quite sure what to do with it after the tragedy. I worked in the women's department, June was the new ladies dress buyer while the company tried to adapt to a changing marketplace.

June would visit the store in Rockefeller Center I'd been assigned to. The other sales people would busily clean and straighten their sections, while praying she wouldn't ask them any questions about sales of a particular line of dresses or handbags.

Me, I waved and said, "Hi, June. How are you?"

My casualness with those in charge drove all rest of the salespeople nuts.

One day, my father stopped into the store. After his inspection of the men's suits to make sure they hung perfectly in line on the racks, he walked over to the ladies side.

"Linny," he called out. "Junie and I are taking you out on Sunday. Be ready at our apartment at eleven."

"Where are we going?" I asked.

"It's a surprise," he said with a grin. "Dress nice."

He turned to leave and once out of sight the other sales girls relaxed and put the Windex and paper towels back in their hiding spot. The jewelry and scarf cases sparkled at least for the next few minutes until a customer came in and decided to smear their greasy fingers all over it.

Sunday morning came. Mom and I both tried to get ready in the small quarters of her one bedroom apartment. She for church and me for my big surprise. I picked out a new skirt I purchased at Rogers Peet with my employee discount, gray with dark red and olive green stripes cut on the bias. With a matching green sweater, I did look adorable, young and thin wearing the latest fashion. Mom pulled a gold necklace out of her dresser drawer and put it around my neck.

"You look so grown up," she said. "Where do you think he's taking you?"

"I have no idea, but I hope it's somewhere fun." A visit to a new museum, lunch at the top of the World Trade Center or even a Broadway show crossed my mind. No matter what Dad chose, I didn't expect to be disappointed.

"Whatever it is I hope you have a good time," Mom said.

I'm grateful for the fact that my parents kept their divorce civil. They never involved their children in their disputes and never held us hostage in them either. June always asked how Mom was doing when I came cross-town for Sunday dinner at their apartment. Mom asked about both their wellbeing when I returned home in the evening. Once Mom asked me to deliver to Dad a past due dental bill for me on my weekly visit but that's the only time I remember being used as the middleman.

Maybe I was wrong that she was looking to get my father back. Mom settled in nicely here making lots of friends at her new church. Church was a solid foundation for her. It always had been. Looking back, church became a solid foundation for me too; I was just too young to recognize it. Occasionally I went with her on Sunday in New York but often I didn't. She didn't mind going alone.

Dad and June were waiting outside their building when I walked up from the bus stop. He hailed a cab and said to the driver, "Penn Station."

When we arrived at the train station, Dad bought three round trip tickets to Belmont Race Track. Off to the horse races we went, Dad's favorite pastime with June and I tagging along. June acted excited but even then I had the impression she was going along for the fun of it, not that she had any real interest in watching a horse race.

At nineteen, I'd never been allowed at a racetrack before though I knew a lot about them from hanging around with Dad. The *Daily Racing Form* must have been delivered to his door every day. I have many memories of him sitting in his favorite chair, with his little stub of a pencil, figuring out his bets for the day's races. No talking allowed while the manual calculations happened. Gambling on horse races took precedent over everything else.

Belmont is a gorgeous place and I took in all the sights and sounds of a new experience. Flowers blooming, perfectly green grass surrounding the neatly combed dirt track. Scores of people milling about, eyes down studying today's racing form trying to decide which thoroughbred would be a winner. I became enthralled with the electricity of the place.

We watched a couple races from our grandstand seats, Dad disappearing a few minutes before the betting windows closed and reappearing when the announcer said, "And they're off!"

As the first horse crossed the finish line, he broke out in a big smile before disappearing again, I assumed to pick up his winnings. June and I snacked on hot dogs and cokes and gossiped about the women wearing elegant hats and men in mismatched outfits passing by.

June had been in my life for almost ten years now and I'd grown to love her excitement at every crazy hairdo or fashion statement that walked by. New York City turned out to be the perfect place for cookoos as she liked to say. June never tried to mother me; she had too much respect for my own mother. So we found common ground in the silly people and places she loved.

"Linny, c'mon," Dad said as the fifth race was announced.

Dutifully I got up and followed him.

Up the steps, across the concourse, down the escalator, around the corners we walked before ending up in the paddock. I don't know the general rules of horse tracks, but how we were able to get so close to the main attraction here was mysterious. Dad glanced over the majestic animals before heading back toward the betting windows.

What I didn't know was I was part of a perfectly choreographed ballet. He walked through a deserted corridor at a frantic pace. A tall, sloppily dressed man in a dirty, wrinkled white shirt and baggy plaid pants limped toward us from the opposite direction. I struggled to keep up and lagged slightly behind Dad.

The two men abruptly stopped in front of one another. The other man looked suspiciously down his nose and over his bushy gray mustache at me.

"My daughter, Linda," Dad said. "This is The Mustache."

"Hello. Nice to meet you," I hesitated not knowing what else appropriate to say to a man whose name was Mustache.

"Escapade to win," said The Mustache.

Dad palmed him some money and ran to place his bet seconds before the window closed. The Mustache disappeared back into the shadows from where he'd come.

Dad's smiled exceptionally big and broad as Escapade crossed the finish line first and by a furlong. So did June. Her years spent by her husband's side at the racetrack taught her to instinctively know the wins from the losses. Somehow I couldn't picture my father emptying his wallet at the dining room table to give June her share of his good luck. Maybe she did love him enough that it made her happy just to see him smile that winning smile.

I had quite the story to tell my college roommates when I returned to school. The most exciting day of summer vacation was spent at the racetrack getting tips from a mysterious man named The

Mustache. Their eyes would widen and their mouths fall open when they heard my tale comparing it to their summers working at Cedar Point amusement park loading a non-stop stream of vacationers onto roller coasters.

Forty years later I view this day quite differently. Dad didn't want to surprise me at all. He wanted to do what he wanted and I was finally old enough to go with him. Why not turn his favorite pastime into a father daughter outing? I never made many demands on either of my parents. I would have been happy going to the fancy ice cream parlor June kept talking about. June probably would have chosen that too. As the youngest and last in line, I typically went with the flow, never sticking my neck out. I was up for any new experience. That made me, in many ways the perfect child to live in between my mother and Dad and June and get along well on both sides of the city.

I suspect that's where the money went for my college education, but maybe he made it back that day and didn't want to share his good fortune on anything more productive than betting on another horse race. Maybe I ended up with a self-absorbed parent who had no idea how to be a parent and had little concern for anyone other than himself.

"Embrace the glorious mess that you are." – Elizabeth Gilbert

CHAPTER SIXTEEN

Exhausted after the long drive home, I dialed June's number before I unpacked the car. The phone rang and rang and rang. I never got June to use an answering machine and now was not the time for any more change other than what was currently being inflicted on her.

"What time is it Richard?" I said to him in the garage.

"Quarter after three," he answered appearing in the doorway with my suitcase.

"I know they feed them early but this seems a little too early for dinner," I said. "Maybe she's getting her hair done."

I made her an appointment before I left. Her hair had been looking kind of ratty lately and in better days I knew bad hair days meant a cranky June.

"Maybe she's playing bingo." He dumped all my dirty clothes in the washing machine. "Stinks like cigarettes," he added.

"I doubt it. Every time I visited her, she was curled up in a ball on her bed." I said. "And you would stink too if you spent a week in June's apartment."

Richard and I settled into our usual banter like I'd never been gone. That was a wonderful benefit of being married for almost thirty years. He filled me in on all the gossip of our 55 plus neighborhood and I showed him all the Thomas Wolfe books in the back of my car. He rolled his eyes like he always did when I brought books home that I had no more room for in the bookcase. He didn't share my love of books; he liked magazines, short, sweet and to the point.

I relaxed quickly now that I was home. Ginger's nails scratched across the tile floor trying to get enough traction to race into my waiting arms. I'd missed her wet kisses and warm snuggles. By the speed of her tail wagging, she missed me too. Forgetting the grief and sorrow of past week however, would take more than a few tummy rubs.

Little by little, I emptied the trunk of the Thomas Wolfe books, June's steel lockbox containing what she considered important papers, like an insurance policy cashed in years ago and Dad's Navy discharge papers that no longer held any importance. The mysterious and scary white box found its way onto my desk. Stacked in my office, I warned Richard not to touch any of it. I had to go through it more thoroughly.

"Why did you bring all this stuff home?" he asked.

"It's old family stuff I couldn't throw away. You know how I am about books," I answered. "But there's that box of papers she left specifically to me. I'm afraid to open it."

"Just open it," he said. "What is there to be afraid of?"

"Oh, I don't know but I feel jittery every time I look at that flimsy old box with my name scribbled on the top. It belongs in a Stephen King novel," I quipped. "I'm really craving a drink right now."

"You didn't bring her booze home, did you?" he asked with an inflection of disbelief. "The cocktail lounge closed here a couple years ago."

"No," I said. "The furniture guy took it. Said he could sell it."

"Are you serious?" Richard asked.

"Every penny we can get, helps," I answered.

About a year after Richard and I moved to Melbourne, Florida away from Delray Beach and June, I found the strength to give up my daily bottle of wine once and for all. What we originally thought was an exciting opportunity started out sour and my drinking only escalated. The sale of the house in Delray fell through four days before the closing and we had already moved into our new, beautiful home on a lake where the birds chirped all day long and deer roamed in the wildlife preserve next door. We started out life here owning two homes and neither of us had a job. What should have been a new exciting adventure turned into anything but and pouring the first glass of wine started at lunchtime when there was nothing left on the daily agenda to do and an eon of anxiety to remove.

Every day fell into a routine. I woke up with a headache, laid around the house nursing it all morning, feeling better around three before pouring a glass of wine. I'd guzzle one down not remembering that the vicious cycle would start all over again.

My drinking habit started in high school when my friends and I would drive to the 7-11, pool our money and ask people going inside to buy us a 6 pack of beer. Some refused and others agreed without giving us back the change. College solidified my habit with Thursday nights downtown at the bars and Friday afternoon fraternity mixers. Once in the working world I came home every night after work and poured myself one, two, three glasses of wine just so I could convince myself I needed to relax.

When I met Richard, our first date was in a tacky Ft. Lauderdale beach bar that served me a glass of white wine in a frosted highball glass with a paper umbrella. He slugged down a V.O. and ginger ale and together we started our relationship as bar flies. He kicked his habit about ten years earlier than me but continued to enable my growing habit by making sure I never ran out of wine.

I was killing myself and I knew it but I felt helpless to stop. Being jobless with no good leads on the horizon, I drank so much Richard started buying me $1.99 rotgut chardonnay at Wal-Mart and I couldn't tell the difference. The buzz felt the same, the buzz that helped to numb my growing anxiety.

Privately without telling anyone, I started praying. Praying to God for help to stop drinking. Each morning I prayed not to reach into the refrigerator and open a bottle of wine. Each afternoon I found myself doing just that, helpless to stop myself. I drank until I finished today's wine bottle and passed out on the sofa with the television blaring. I was a patient person but at this time in my life, I wished I wasn't. I wanted to take this crutch called alcohol, break it over my knee and toss it out the window. I'd had enough. I knew in my heart when the right time arrived, I would be more than strong; I would be invincible.

One day I went to the kitchen to start cooking dinner. I opened the refrigerator and took out the chicken, potatoes and some fresh broccoli, set them on the counter and closed the refrigerator door. My habitual reach for the wine bottle didn't happen that day. I took a deep breath and started chopping.

That my usual glass of wine wasn't sitting next to my dinner plate didn't go unnoticed.

"No wine tonight?" Richard asked with a forkful of potatoes hanging halfway between his plate and his mouth.

"I'm trying to quit," I answered.

"Want me to throw out all the bottles in the pantry? I don't want you to be tempted," he said.

Richard knocked his alcohol habit many years ago. That I wasn't able to kick mine had turned into a huge source of tension in our marriage. When I poured my wine, everything else stopped. I didn't want to walk the dog, play Scrabble, Richard's favorite game, or leave the house for a dinner out. My wine in hand, I settled in on the sofa in front of the television until I felt numbness from the tips of my fingers to the end of my toes. Then I passed out.

"Not yet. I'll be okay," I said as my hands shook.

"I'm proud of you," he answered.

The long, hard road to sobriety began. I hadn't planned to stop drinking that day. I had simply been patient. God chose that time and place to answer my prayer. I am forever grateful He did.

Without alcohol, my usual morning headache lasted all-day and night for a month. I walked around the house in slow motion, often nauseous, aching from head to toe. I talked to God a lot because if I didn't I would have just uncorked a bottle and taken a swig. But I didn't.

When my energy returned, and I sat down in front of the television at the end of a long, full day, without a glass of wine, I realized how big a crutch alcohol had been for me. So many books and magazines I hadn't read, so many movies I passed out in the middle of, so many novels and stories I hadn't taken the time to write. The world suddenly became an interesting place to explore. I no longer needed to sit down and relax with a drink after a long day of doing nothing.

If Richard and I had stayed in Delray near June and our weekly dinners out continued, would I have ever made the leap to sobriety? Richard's sobriety started in 2000 and June continued to buy him a bottle of Seagram's V.O. for years. She had it at the ready for him and offered to make him a drink whenever we visited her home. His mixer of ginger ale kept an unopened bottle of Robert Mondavi chardonnay company in her refrigerator.

I'll never know if June truly believed her drinking habit wasn't harmful. She could never stop at one and never let me either, always pouring me another glass and placing it in my hand. Not that I had the willpower to stop at one, but with a little encouragement I might have tried. Looking backward, I don't believe I would have developed the desire to stop as long as June and I were hanging out together. She wasn't the only factor but she was a big part of my habit.

Thank God she never tried to get me hooked on cigarettes.

After a long hot shower to scrub the last of the stench of smoke from my body, my muscles released a tiny, tiny bit of the tension.

I picked up the phone and called June again.

"Hi, June. It's Linda." For years I called her and never identified myself. She knew the sound of my voice. After the first time she asked who was calling, I started adding my introduction.

"Linda," she growled. "Where are you? I need you."

"I'm at home June. What do you need?" I calmly asked.

"You abandoned me! You and Richard left me all alone. I hate it here."

The rock I now carried around in the pit of my stomach suddenly felt five pounds heavier than it had a few moments ago.

"You have my phone number. I wrote it in your book on the nightstand," Suddenly I became the mother again, trying to calm and pacify the child. "You can call me anytime you want."

"There's no one here for me to talk to," she whined.

"What about the ladies you sit with in the dining room? They seemed pleasant," I said.

"They don't understand. I need to talk to *you*." I could hear the frustration and agitation in her voice. She seemed to be missing our chat sessions but for very different reasons, drinks and cigarettes included.

"Okay, I'll call you tomorrow and we can talk." I crossed my fingers my pathetic response would ease her anxiety, a tactic that had worked for me sporadically in the past. Right now anything was worth another shot.

"Okay. I'll like that. I love you."

I heaved a sign of relief and before I could say I love you too, the phone went dead. This pattern of anger and docility had become June's new normal. I never knew which I would get when I spoke to her and I never knew what I said to switch her from one to the other.

The town Richard and I moved to is called Viera, a Slavic word for faith. After conversations like this one, I took a deep breath and relaxed in knowing I had found my faith here. My mother raised us in a Presbyterian church, which gave me a foundation but not a faith. I had to find that on my own and God saw fit to introduce me to it here, in Viera. That's why I found it so difficult to go back to a place and a life where that didn't exist for me any longer.

After a week away, a stack of bills waited for me in my office alongside the things from June's home, I dumped there. I sliced open envelope after envelope of bills needing to be paid and neatly stacked them in the corner of my desk. I ripped the junk mail in half, and filed away the property tax notice without even looking at it. I crammed the trash into an overflowing wastebasket.

All that was left for me to do now was discover the contents of the infamous yet unassuming box with my name written on the top. After all I saw in June's closets and cupboards during the past week, I wanted to feel June had run out of surprises for me. An unpleasant gnawing inside me thought she saved the best or maybe the worst revelation for last.

"Richard," I shouted. "I'm going to go through the box. Don't bother me for awhile." Diet Coke in hand, I steeled my nerves to take the plunge.

"I won't. Shut the door," he replied.

I told Richard about the box during a frequent phone conversation while I was away. He was more curious than I, but knew the box was hands off for him until I had the courage to share it. I heard the telltale sounds of a baseball game playing on the television in the other room.

Sitting on the floor, I tried to make myself comfortable which was impossible. My back ached and my knees creaked no matter what position I put them in. I stared at the box for a good long time before mustering up the courage to lift the lid. After taking a long deep breath, I slowly removed it waiting for a snake to crawl out or a creepy Jack in the Box head to pop up and scare the daylights out of me. I ended up only to be confronted with that distinctive June smell, not of a sweet perfume but a musty, moldy odor finished off with a dose of stale cigarettes. The headache that had released its grip somewhere on the turnpike between Boca Raton and Ft. Pierce instantly returned.

Greeting cards of every size, shape and color lay scattered in front of me. I reached for a black one on top of the pile.

With Sympathy, it said in fancy cursive silver letters. I reached for another one.

Thinking of you during this difficult time.

My heart skipped a few beats and my head felt dizzy. She saved all the sympathy cards and letters she received when my father died twenty-five years ago and had put them in a box for me. I swallowed back the bile rising in my throat. The sickening feeling I carried with me the day of Dad's funeral had returned in full force.

I shuffled a few more cards out of the pile to reveal some letters. Several were in my mother's handwriting, one from my grandmother and a few from my sisters. On others I recognized the return addresses of my Aunt Mary, my father's sister. Some envelopes said "Paul" written by June. At the very bottom, I uncovered my parent's divorce decree and Dad and June's marriage license.

I could no longer hold back the force of the tears welling in my eyes. Pushing the precious letters aside, I reached for a tissue not wanting any teardrops to fall on the paper that had been cared for all these years and saved for me. Why? I now had to find out.

I opened an envelope and began to read.

"Oh, what a tangled web we weave, when first we practice to deceive." – Sir Walter Scott

CHAPTER SEVENTEEN

Monday, January 2nd 1967

Dear Mr. Wright

The time is growing close…and somehow I can't let you leave without some kind of a letter…I wouldn't be "true to type" would I? I want to wish you all the good things of life.

I've been so happy for you, that I have put my own feelings in the background…and now…that the day is almost here, I find a lump in my throat, and the inability to be articulate or even to say "Au Revoir".

It's been a good five years with you…in a big Store… where I never could have survived without you…without your understanding or your perceptive awareness. You are refreshing this world of Cold Corporate Thinking...sort of like a signal of Hope, and as you go from one plateau to another, carrying people on your shoulder all the way up, the last stop can only be at the very top of the ladder.

Your humble quiet strength, your homespun, fun-loving humor, your compassion...your brilliant strokes of creative and imaginative thinking...your priceless chuckles...your long range vision...your loyalties...and your Golden Rule Philosophy by which you live...all of these have warmed our hearts and especially mine.

Your worry and concern for us when occasionally we "lose our touch"...your courage to stand by us through rough days...never once succumbing to panic, never forsaking your principles, for immediate rewards...your integrity.

All of these things are the "Measure of a Man."

And so... Good Luck, Good Health...and God Bless you.

Marguerite

Mixed in with the sympathy cards, was a tattered brown envelope labeled 'Divorce Papers' written in my father's handwriting. Attached to it was this typewritten letter from Dad's secretary at the May Company in Cleveland, Marguerite. We knew her, heard her name often. She loved to fuss over us kids too whenever we came to the office to visit.

It caught my eye because of the math calculations in red ink Dad had done on the back of the envelope. He might have been figuring out the amount of his last paycheck, subtracting the child support he owed for that month of January or he might have been figuring what he had to pay his divorce lawyer. Those numbers say to me, he didn't feel remorse about leaving an employee who clearly loved working for him. He had a new job and a new life to start in Seattle and he wanted to move on. That was my father, waste no time and get going.

The overstuffed envelope behind the secretary's goodbye contained legal documents, all typewritten on onionskin paper, a kind of paper I hadn't used since high school. The see-through crinkly paper showed its age, freckled with brown spots around the edges. The words, however, were clear as the day the secretary typed them on her Royal manual typewriter.

I could see ink and handwriting through one thin piece. I hadn't seen anything written by Dad's hand in years but his big loopy 'P', long tail of a 'y' and fat 't's crossed at the very top, were easily recognizable. I felt comfort in knowing he had touched these papers and they were now mine regardless of the painful topic of divorce.

A wave of uncertainty washed over me. Was I intruding? Did I want to go to a place I pushed out of my mind decades ago? I believe a marriage belongs only to the two people in it. If that union is unsuccessful, it's not the result of any one else's actions and that includes the children. Did I need to know after all these years the secrets I might find inside these crinkly, yellowed pages? I hesitated before unfolding the delicate paper. It was a letter written by my father to the court in Cleveland.

March 15, 1967
Common Pleas Court
Dept. of Domestic Relations
Cleveland, Ohio
Dear Mr. McCay,

This is to confirm our telephone conversation of Wednesday, March 15, 1967 concerning your card to me in regard to a divorce action under case No. 937487.

I am not contesting the divorce and do consider the plaintiff a good mother.

Yours very truly,

Paul H. Wright

Years ago, I lost interest in the stress and long hours of working the in the retail business. The structure of the department store had changed dramatically from the one Dad and June knew and had groomed me for. Over my working years I'd been banished from fashion lines, not having much of an aptitude for it, and sent to the hard lines section of the department store, china, crystal, and small appliances. In the early 1990's I went back to school and got a degree in accounting before taking and passing the exam to become a Certified Public Accountant.

As I read this first letter, my analytical accounting mind kicked into high gear. Dad left The May Company and Cleveland in January. In March, the divorce wasn't yet final. The day my mother delivered the news Dad and June were married was in May. The next document I read turned out to be the official legal divorce decree with the raised seal of the court. I unfolded the stiff legal document.

First and foremost the children's complete names were listed along with our ages. I was always last, a position I've grown used to over the years. I'm still the little sister and sometimes even the baby sister, which grates on me like nail on a chalkboard. Even my last name starts with a "W", which in school put me at the end of the line. Used to being last both alphabetically and numerically, I learned to practice a life of patience. To this day, waiting at the doctor's office or at motor vehicles, or the Wal-Mart checkout line, doesn't bother me. I've spent a lifetime being last. Not letting the order of things bother me, I kept reading.

According to the legal papers, my mother received $500 a month alimony, which dropped by half each time a child entered college. She also received $150 per month per child in child support. Each child's portion was eliminated when starting college. This was a large sum of money each month in 1967. Once *I* graduated from college it all stopped.

Many things in my parent's divorce hinged on me and me growing up as soon as possible. Susan was in college, so her half of things dropped off before the divorce was final. Martha, a senior in high school heading to college, would be contributing her reduction of payments in a few months. Steve and I were the holdouts because we hadn't even made it into high school yet.

Next came the visitation rules, three weeks in the summer and a week to start after Christmas Day. Dad got to claim all four of us as dependents on his tax return. He quit claimed deeded the big house in the suburbs of Pepper Pike to my mother, a house he paid $60,000 in 1961 when he took a job at the May Company and we moved from Minneapolis. Along with the house, Mom got Dad's 1964 Ford, the one she drove to pick up June for dinner all those years ago.

What suddenly struck me was how my parents both followed these instructions to the letter. At least they did from my perspective.

Steve and I flew to wherever Dad and June lived at the time, for exactly three weeks each summer. Once he moved to New York, we spent the week between Christmas and New Years tromping around the big city in the snow and slush. Mom never complained his check was late or forbid us from speaking to him on the phone whenever he called. It took a long time for Mom to move on with her life emotionally, but neither of my parents ever held us kids as bait against the other. For that I'm grateful.

I looked for the date on the final divorce decree. April 27, 1967. My father hadn't wasted any time marrying June in May.

The revelation of the close proximity of dates between Dad's second marriage to June and the date of the final divorce bubbled up another unpleasant memory of being in New York and cleaning out my mother's apartment after she moved to a nursing home permanently.

The week in New York with my sisters, my brother and his wife had been grueling to say the least. Susan, as the oldest, insisted she knew best about everything. I had spent the most time in New York City while I lived with my mother during my college years and knew my way around. I was still the baby sister and incapable of making any proper decisions in the others eyes.

We spent the week arguing over who should get Mom's china or her favorite painting of Canadian geese which hung over the sofa. No one wanted the professional high school graduation photos Mom had framed and hung on the wall. Other than that we didn't agree on much.

So when Susan, Steve and Karen left early to go home to Dayton, Martha and I heaved a huge sigh of relief.

"Where do you think Mom's Christmas ornaments are? I'd like to have some of those old glass bulbs we put on the tree as kids," I said. "I know they're still here somewhere."

"Did you look in the closet?" Martha asked.

I stuck my head in the hall closet still jam packed with coats, boots and boxes. I didn't see anything labeled 'Xmas' so I started taking lids off boxes, watching the thick layers of dust swirl beneath my nose.

"Martha. Here's some old letters. See what you find in there," I coughed.

My fascination with hand written correspondence started years ago. Whenever Dad went on buying trips to Europe, Mom would buy the flimsy, blue airmail stationery at the post office for us to write to him. I crammed every last available inch of paper with an accounting of everything I did in school or Girl Scouts. He would send us back fancy French greeting cards. The thrill of finding these exquisite envelopes in the mailbox sent me over the moon as a child. I couldn't pass up looking through this old box of faded letters belonging to Mom.

I handed the sagging brown box to Martha and continued the search for the decorations. I finally hit pay dirt in the far corner of the closet under several boxes of old clothes marked 'Goodwill'. That was my mother, always putting off until tomorrow what should have been done five years ago. Whatever we left in the apartment was headed to charity anyway, we made those arrangements to lessen the headache of disposing of furniture and clothing we had no use for.

Brushing the dust from my hair, I carried the Christmas stuff out to the living room where Martha sat reading a letter from the box.

"You might want to read this," she said wide eyed while gasping for breath. She handed me an old faded envelope addressed to Mom at the big house in Cleveland where we lived pre-divorce, written in my father's hand.

The only few snippets I remember on the page were first, "You teach the children good hygiene habits but don't follow them yourself." My mother's desire and ability to care for her physical body started long before she grew into old age. That's another reason all her children were embarrassed by her presence. She didn't know how to dress herself, brush her hair or have the energy to brush her teeth. What we didn't know in our younger years was she suffered from depression that went untreated for most of her life. Back then depression wasn't a popular buzzword like it is today. Mom suffered physically and we could only see her as a mother we were ashamed of.

The second and most powerful line on the page was "I want you to know, I'm not a philanderer." I can still see the words written in my father's script.

Martha looked at me and I at her and at that moment we decided to destroy the letter my mother had saved for over thirty years. Nothing good would come out of anyone else reading it or from saving it.

After all these years that time and place came rushing back to me. In a second I put together a timeline I discovered in the contents of the box June left for me, that my father was not the same man who drilled the Golden Rule into his children's heads. *Do unto others, as you would have others do unto you.* The vision I carried of him in my mind shattered. He was a liar. Maybe he didn't lie to his children, but he did to my mother to pacify his own ego.

What other secrets lived inside this box of letters June wanted me to have? She loved Paul and I doubt she set out to destroy him in my mind. June met me as a little girl and must have wanted me to decide as an adult how the actions of others created the relationship of trust we grew into together. I pulled out another envelope.

"Forget what hurt you, but never forget what it taught you." - Anonymous

CHAPTER EIGHTEEN

December 7, 1974

Dear Hath,

I have a couple of Christmas "presents" for you. I hope you'll accept them; they are all I have at the moment.

One - Linda will be home on the 13th. We are going to Detroit the 20th until the 25th, but feel free to have her with you whenever you wish. She'll be working as a file clerk while she's here - but her evenings and weekends are yours, if you want them.

Second - I've been saying for several years that our divorce was probably the best thing that ever happened to me. I really mean that!!! For you, now, I say thank God you had the

courage to make the break. I never could have and we probably
both would have lost.

I love it here in New York. Life is lovelier for me than it
has been for many, many years.

Thank you. My best to you and June and a
Merry Christmas.

Sallie

As I read this letter from my mother to my father that June had kept all these years in my box, I felt I was being used as a piece of property to be given or taken away at will. A child's view of his or her parent's divorce is a far different thing than that of anyone else. Stepping back into this time through the words of my mother opened up wounds I kept stitched shut for decades.

As I sat on the floor of my warm and cozy office space in a spare bedroom, memories flooded forward and overflowed until I couldn't hold them back any longer.

* * *

My senior year in college was nothing short of a freaking nightmare. My long time boyfriend broke up with me in September and all the fun I expected to have as a senior on the brink of real adult life, flitted away in a fog of disbelief.

I'd gone to college four years earlier with no real plan in mind. I only wanted to escape my mother's grip and be free to do whatever I wanted. No curfew, no rules. High school classes had been easy for me, though I wasn't a scholar I graduated in the top 20% of my class.

I was accepted to every college I applied to including a few pricey private ones I was not allowed to attend. I chose Bowling Green State University arriving there one chilly fall day in 1973 without any idea of what college life would turn out to be.

Studying had never been my strong suit while in college, drinking had been, and my grades reflected that. Somehow I managed to stay enrolled. Between Friday afternoon "teas" with the fraternity boys and Thursday nights downtown bar hopping, I managed to find an excuse to drown my sorrows seven days a week.

Looking back, I fell into the trap all my friends did at that time. We were college girls fully expecting to start exciting careers of some kind at the end of our college degrees but secretly wanting to be the one blowing out the candle at the sorority ceremony meaning we'd been lavaliered or pinned or even engaged. We were the generation of women caught in the middle. While strides had been made so we could enter any profession we wanted, our upbringing as young girls included as our primary mission in life to get married and have children. Prior generations of women never dreamed those two choices; a career and a family would ever meet. For me however, they intersected and I became caught at the crossroads.

Walking across the football field to pomp and circumstance followed by walking down the aisle to the wedding march was no longer going to be the start to my life. I was devastated. Every time I watched one of my sorority sisters blow out that candle, I wanted to cry. I was so jealous I never got a chance to be the center of attention, as soon as the candle was extinguished; I bolted back to my room and let the others gush the newly pinned sister. We sang an Elvis song, *"Only Fools Rush*

In". If I paid more attention to the lyrics, I might not have been in such a hurry to rush into a marriage that was strictly selfish and superficial. At the time I didn't know anything other than selfish. For once in my life, I wanted the world to be about me and only me.

Graduation day fast approached and what was coming next frightened me. I had a rough time lining up a job but finally landed one at Gimbels in Pittsburgh in their retail management training program. How I got the job I don't know but I suspect my father pulled some strings with his years of department store connections. People I met at Gimbels still remembered Dad from when he was the ladies coat buyer in 1955, the year I was born. If the stack of rejection letters piling up in my mailbox were any indication, I would not be able to land any kind of job by myself.

Excited by the prospect of heading into my great unknown, I invited my parents to my graduation, and reserved them both hotel rooms at the local Holiday Inn. My sorority sisters had done the same thing for their families and our excitement waiting for the big day was electric. We'd miss our days of silly sisterhood pranks, late night study halls and pledge activations but we were all ready to move forward. Packed and ready to start a new chapter, all I had left to do was pick up my cap and gown.

One afternoon, I just got back to my room from a management class I'd be lucky to end up with a D, the phone in my room rang.

"Hello."

"Hi, Linda. It's June."

June? Why was June calling me? She never called me. We talked on the phone periodically but only because she answered when I called Dad. She never initiated a phone call to me. My stomach fluttered.

"I'm calling about your graduation. It's on June 11th right?" she asked.

"Yep. I reserved your hotel room for Friday and Saturday nights," I said.

"That's what I'm calling about. Your father and I aren't going to be able to make it," she said.

My heart sank to the floor and my legs turned to rubber. I should have known he'd back out. Dad sounded excited about it when I called to invite him and June a few months ago. I should have remembered that for him, work and his Junie came before Linny. A men's suit vendor must have invited them for a free weekend in the Hamptons. That's where the 'in' people from the city went in the summer.

"How come?" I asked.

"Paul has some other obligations for work on that day." June replied. "You understand, don't you?"

I answered yes because that's what I'd been trained by both of my parents to do, never disagree with someone older and in an authority position. I did not understand. I will never understand why neither of my parents ever showed any interest in participating in the special moments in my life.

This was my college graduation, the only one I would ever have. I was the youngest and last. Once and for all, I was relieving both of my parents of the financial burden of tuition, room and board, alimony and child support. I figured that was cause for celebration not just for me but also for both of them. Obviously I'll never understand why Dad didn't share in that triumph with me, or have the guts to make that call himself.

I was soon to find out my mother didn't share in the glory of graduation with me either.

On graduation eve she flew to Toledo from New York and rented a car for the short hop down to Bowling Green. I met her at the hotel.

"When's your father getting here?" she asked.

She never asked about Dad's plans prior to her arrival and I saw no reason to inform her of them either. My parents were divorced after all.

"He's not coming." I answered and then I waited for her reaction.

"What do you mean he's not coming?" she asked.

"I don't know why. June called to tell me they couldn't make it." I said. "I'm supposed to understand."

Mom stopped unpacking her suitcase.

"Well, then who am I supposed to sit with?" she demanded to know.

My mouth fell open and I stared in disbelief at this woman who pretended to be my mother.

"Whoever is in the seat next to you on the bleachers," I answered.

"Call Carol German or your friend, Stacy Stout. Their parents must be here," she said.

Mom still remembered the names of girls I hung around with in high school. Both had come to Bowling Green State University with me but when they left me out when selecting their dorms during freshman summer orientation, I lost contact with them. BGSU had over

15,000 students while I was there. It's a big place. I didn't run into them in my daily schedule and sorority commitments.

"Mom. I lost touch with both of them long ago. I wouldn't know where to find them," I said.

My temper began to flare and my blood began to boil. This time was supposed to be about me. It was not. It was about everyone else in my family. I was always the afterthought. I was supposed to 'understand' every time I got pushed to the back of the line. I tagged along with Mom to Susan's college graduation at Wittenberg. Martha graduated early in December and then proceeded to get married to her first husband so a wedding substituted for a cap and gown. Steve refused to go to either his high school or college ceremony. None of my siblings found it important to show up for my special day either.

"I've got to finish packing up my stuff. I'll come back around six and we can get some dinner." My ears burned and I couldn't listen to her unreasonable blather any longer.

Mom didn't answer and I opened the door to the room and walked down the hall. I made a slow, labored death march across campus back to the sorority house, wiping the tears from my face first with one hand and then the other for the entire mile. I snuck in the side door and prayed no one would see my red and swollen face. Luckily for me, all my sisters were out with their families enjoying the attention that a soon to be college graduate deserved for their accomplishment. The house was unusually empty and quiet.

I finished putting the last of my college remembrances into my trunk; a hand made paddle from my sorority little sister, a traditional gift. I wrapped it in a well-worn towel after four years of being used for a variety of things not only to dry off after showering. I'd take them to my new home, in Pittsburgh, a city where I knew no one, and make do until I could hopefully earn enough money to furnish an apartment the way I wanted.

Not wanting to be late and face more of my mother's unreasonable logic, I made the return trek back to the hotel. Mom waited for me in the lobby. We walked next door to the Golden Kettle and ate in silence. After dinner she drove me back to the sorority house.

"Can you give me a tour?" she asked.

"Sure," I said hoping the house would be equally as empty as it had been this afternoon so I wouldn't have to make any awkward introductions.

I got lucky once again.

After I showed her the kitchen and living room downstairs, and the showers and laundry room on my floor, Mom sat down in my college issued desk chair and said, "I need to talk to you."

I sat crossed legged on the floor, nervously running my fingers through the orange and red shag carpet that I detested the entire year I walked on it. The best rooms in the sorority house, those with most windows and closest to the stairwell had the ugliest carpets. The trade off, I suppose, for seniority in the organization.

"I know this is a big moment for you, graduating from college." She took in a deep breath. "But you're going to run into a lot of roadblocks especially living in a new city. Stronger people than you have tried and failed."

My face dropped toward the floor and the disgusting rug. I couldn't speak or look her in the eye. Mom rambled on about how easy my life had been up until now, and I'd better toughen up if I expected to survive in the real world. I closed my ears and my mind to the rest.

From the day I left home for college, I took care of myself. I'll admit, I didn't always do such a bang up job, but I certainly wasn't going to ever turn up on her doorstep homeless and penniless in defeat. While my parents covered my college costs, I worked in the sorority house kitchen washing dishes to cover my dues and provide some drinking money. I had a substantial bank account that I built up by working summers and after school while in high school. Grandma sent me $500 as a down payment on a used car for a graduation gift. I could get myself started in an apartment without going broke.

I was never going home again, I made up my mind about that a long time ago. If that's what my mother was afraid of, all she had to do was ask me. I could have saved us both the time and effort she invested in a hurtful and useless lecture on the eve of my journey into adulthood.

Forty years later however, I've never forgotten those words. They're what got me to where I am today, in a marriage that has lasted for more than thirty years, financially secure, living a happy, peaceful life that I love. On that day, at that moment, my mother reduced me to less than nothing. She ripped what little sliver of a soul I had left and ground it into that pitiful orange and red shag carpet.

On what should have been an occasion filled with tears of happiness had been reduced to rubble. Without any idea why my father chose not to participate in this grand affair, there I stood facing the future all alone.

"Better to fight for something, than live for nothing." -George S. Paton

CHAPTER NINETEEN

Happy Valentine's Day

My Dearest Paul,

When you first came to the May Co., I knew I liked you. Little did I know we were destined to spend our lives together. It's been almost 21 years of perfection —- thanks to you. I wouldn't trade places with anyone I know, because with you I have it all! You are the kindest, most loving, intelligent and sensitive person in the world —- and I love you and every minute we have together. You also don't let me get away with too much and that's for the best!

Love,

Junie

After college, I lived and worked in Pittsburgh for several years on my own. I made friends and I got promoted to assistant buyer at Gimbels. I pulled down a meager salary even with my new position; I dated a little and mostly hung out with a group of buyers and managers from work. I enjoyed my independent life but emotionally needed something more.

On April 9th, 1980, I slipped and fell on some ice and cut open my lip with one of my teeth. I remember the date because it was my mother's birthday and it's the day I decided I no longer wanted to put up with the cold, snowy winters. I started my search for a job in Florida.

My best friend from elementary school, Georgia and her husband, Terry, moved to Miami the day after their wedding a few years earlier. Dad and June moved to Tampa after leaving the Big Apple and doing a short stint in Chicago. I had some options to live near friends and family, which is what I really wanted after three years of unsuccessfully trying to integrate myself into a strange city.

I arrived in Tampa to stay with Dad and June for a few days before heading to Miami. They had a beautiful but small condo on a high floor with sweeping views overlooking Tampa Bay. By small I mean only one bedroom. The red sofa was no more and I slept on the couch in the living room. Maggie and Molly greeted me at the door, older and fatter but just as feisty.

The first three days I spent in Tampa were filled with Dad driving me around to job interviews at local department stores. He had a new Cadillac after years of living in New York without the need for a car. I told him what time my interview was and where and he got me there with time to spare. He relished in the task of driving Junie around town to all of her appointments. In the days before GPS he knew just where to go. Retirement seemed to suit him.

I met with people at Maas Brothers and Robinson's in St. Petersburg knowing a convincing interview wasn't my strength. All my life I'd been kind of shy until I went to college and a boy put a drink in my hand. These people were only interested in my job skills not my dancing ability. I struggled to convince them I'd be a good fit in their organization and I left every interview not feeling very optimistic I would find a new home here.

The only television in the apartment was in the master bedroom. Dad sat in an uncomfortable barrel chair to watch it in the evening. June stretched out on the bed, wrapping her hair in orange foam rollers. I usually sat on the floor with the dogs.

One morning I took his place in the his favorite chair while he read the paper in the living room and June fussed with her coffee and the dishes in the kitchen.

I don't remember what I was watching, some blathering morning talk show, when the conversation in the living room suddenly became much more interesting.

"We'll leave for the racetrack around eleven," I heard my father say.

"We are not," June answered. "You spend too much money there. We can't afford it."

"Junie. We're going to the track. We're not broke. Stop it," he said.

"No, we're not," the volume of her voice raised several notches.

"You aren't telling me what to do," Dad answered back.

June started into a tirade about everything wrong under the sun. So many things flew out of her mouth, I couldn't keep track. Dad burst through the bedroom door, flung open the closet, rummaged around for a bit before removing a suitcase. It landed with a thump on the bed.

My eyes glued to the television, I stole a glance in his direction every few seconds. He never looked up or made eye contact with me. Whatever was on his mind, I never saw him so laser focused. This was turning out to be better than any lawsuit in front of Judge Wapner on *The People's Court*. I took after Dad in that I inherited his temperament. He never blew up, always calm and collected. The story goes that his father and stepmother argued all the time growing up and he hated listening to them. He made up his mind not to repeat that in his own home and refused to raise his voice. He simply walked away from an argument. I'd seen him do this to Mom too, years ago before they divorced. She'd scream and waive her hands and he'd continue to watch television, ignoring her. I'd never seen or heard the two lovebirds toss barbs like I did that day.

June's scratchy voice permeated every room. Dad said nothing in return. He quietly emptied a dresser drawer into the suitcase, folded some pants and shirts still on their hangers and closed the case. He picked up his things and marched, suitcase in hand, toward the front door.

Wailing as loud and as piercing as a police siren came next, similar to the sound June made years ago when she thought she had a bug crawling through her hair, but sharper with a hint of scratchy gravel. A few more harsh words exchanged between the two of them. The crying stopped. Dad came back into the bedroom put down the suitcase and said,

"Linny. Be ready in a half hour. We're going to the track."

I changed my clothes, put on some makeup and was ready to go right on time without saying a single word to either of them. I took my spot on the soft plush leather back seat of the big, white Cadillac. June, all dolled up in a new blue dress and her favorite strand of pearls, took her seat in the front. Dad drove us to the racetrack in silence but he'd gotten his way. I looked forward to a day at the track. I could now place a bet or two since I'd surpassed legal age a couple years ago. June and I would pick out a horse by a name that we liked and I'd walk up to the betting window acting like I'd done it a thousand times before. Dad probably had a new local tipster waiting in the wings.

Dad hit it big that day betting on the horses. June and I were ordered to scour the seats to pick up losing betting slips thrown away on the dirty concrete floors. We stuffed our purses full of crumpled papers dirtied with footprints and coffee stains. He needed them as evidence for the accountant to offset the gambling win on his tax return. My father smiled at his good luck and I didn't hear June make a peep the entire drive home. She'd never won an argument with him and she knew better than to pick a fight with him when his pockets were full of money.

"What lies behind us and what lies before us are tiny matters compared to what lies within us." - Ralph Waldo Emerson

CHAPTER TWENTY

6/11/1992

Dear Linda and Richard,

At long last there are beautiful faces to match your names I hear so often. We loved meeting you to share June's delicious meal and hope our paths will cross again.

Your friendship with June is very precious to her and I almost need to thank you. Well not almost, I do thank you for your constant caring.

Have a good summer.

Fondly,

Nan

Shortly after my trip to Tampa, I took a job at Jordan Marsh in Boca Raton and moved to Florida. Nothing about my move went smoothly for me. The moving companies were all on strike when it was time for me to leave Pittsburgh. I packed my Kermit the Frog green, Ford Pinto, on the auto train and it rebelled all the way to Miami from the all bouncing around on the ride from Washington, D.C. to Sanford, Florida. My furniture still hadn't arrived at my roach infested apartment when I landed in the hospital for a week needing surgery for an abscess.

Dad and June waited until things had settled down a little in my life before deciding to move to Boca to join me. Though they never said it, I'm sure this was their way of protecting themselves by living near one of their children, as they got older. I doubt their decision had anything to do with helping me put my struggles behind me.

I gave up on my dream of being a part of a close-knit family. My roots were going to grow where I wanted them to, not where my parents decided to live. Florida gave me a rough start but I loved the freedom and the sunshine here. After Dad's recovery from an aortic aneurysm, they suddenly realized they weren't getting any younger. Without asking, they decided living near me was an investment in their old age.

By the time Dad and June moved to Boca, I'd met and moved in with Richard, the love of my life. I met him while at Jordan Marsh, he sold furniture and I managed the luggage, toys and sporting goods departments next door. My job at Jordan Marsh lasted only six months.

I didn't see eye to eye with the management team, so I began searching for a new job as soon as the grueling Christmas holiday ended. I found Richard's cute and charming smile on my way to the ladies room, which was tucked in the back of the furniture department. Luckily I moved on to a store manager position at F.A.O.Schwarz in Ft. Lauderdale, which was more to my liking and moved in with Richard at the same time.

Dad and June bought a townhouse in Boca about five miles away from where we lived. It was a spacious three bedroom, a patio in the back and a garage for Dad's new white Cadillac. It came with plenty of green space to walk the beloved, black standard poodle, Shana.

Then I got engaged.

At thirty-one years old, I wasn't going to plan any ordinary wedding. Richard, being thirteen years older than me, had walked down the aisle twice before. It wouldn't be any ordinary marriage either but as a first time bride, the wedding was going to be my way. I planned it myself and I paid for it myself.

We picked the date, Valentine's Day. The fourteenth of February fell on a Saturday so why not and who doesn't want to escape from the cold and frozen north to Florida in the middle of winter? Our family and friends were told well in advance to make their travel arrangements early for our big day.

My thought process had always been black and white; no fuzzy gray exists in my world. That means I love traditions, like wearing a garter and throwing the bouquet totally believing the person who catches it is the next to be married. The saying something old, something new, something borrowed, something blue, lived firmly planted in my mind. I wanted a classic wedding to start an unconventional marriage.

This was the 1980's and I chose not to change my name, or to use any hyphens either. I kept the name Wright opting not to take Richard's name, Jaunich. To most people I knew, this was groundbreaking for the time. I made no visit to the Social Security office and to this day, I still carry a copy of my marriage license in my wallet. For a few years I had to show it to employers, doctors, and at the bank to open a joint checking account. No one believed I could get away with such a bold move.

Again in my life I chose a path that led to a crossroad, I wanted to join what was normal and accepted with a bold, new idea. These are the kinds of things that spark change in this world even though I hardly saw myself as a trailblazer. I was a bride on a mission and worked feverishly on planning every detail by myself, no hovering mother of the bride existed in my world. That was fine by me. This was my time to be in the spotlight.

At the drugstore, I bought every available bride magazine and the wedding planning began in earnest. It would be a small affair, fifty guests sailing up and down the Intracoastal on a classic Trumpy yacht that supposedly belonged to Marilyn Monroe and Joe DiMaggio. The story is sketchy at best, and it's far more likely Miss Monroe spent time on the Presidential Trumpy yacht, Sequoia, with John F. Kennedy than actually owned one herself. We certainly weren't partying on the Sequoia but a cousin of the famous boat was equally as impressive.

Prince Andrew and Fergie had recently married and she carried a beautiful crescent shaped bouquet of pale yellow roses and gardenias with a cascade of white lilies on one end. I only had to say to the florist,

"I want a bouquet like Fergie's. Use pink roses though, that's my color scheme," I said. "And no gardenias. I'm allergic.

I got exactly what I wanted, white orchids, pink roses and lily of the valley. Fergie's bouquet included a touch of myrtle, as do all royal wedding arrangements for good luck. I'm not sure if the florist added any myrtle for me but since my marriage lasted over thirty years and Fergie's didn't, either way it worked out for the best.

I ordered the required corsages for our mothers, both my sisters and June. June hadn't attended either of my sister's weddings since the wounds of divorce were still too fresh. Neither she nor Dad came to Martha's second marriage to Tom. My guess is they gave one of those "you understand, don't you?" excuses because all of the rest of us showed up, including Mom.

June was coming to my wedding though. With great enthusiasm, she called me on the phone to ask my preferences for her own dress.

"Linda, your father's taking me shopping for my dress for your wedding. What's your color scheme?" she asked.

"Pink," I answered.

"Pink's the perfect color for Valentine's Day. What's your mother wearing?" she asked.

"I don't know," I answered. "I'm not worried that everyone blends. Wear what you like and makes you happy."

"I found this new shop selling designer dresses at deep discounts. We're going to check it out tomorrow." That was June. Always the ladies dress buyer looking for a bargain.

When it came time for me to pick out my own dress, I took Martha. She and Tom came to Florida for a visit so I talked her into going with me. I came armed with pictures of dresses I thought I'd like and presented them to the bridal consultant at a small shop across the street from the mall. I'm not the froo froo type so no beading or sequins and certainly not a long flowing train.

I tried on the dresses I had loved in the magazines and none of them fit the bill. A woman knows instinctively when she's put on the perfect wedding dress and I was no different.

"This is a bridesmaid dress but we can order it in white if you like it," the saleswoman said.

I slipped into an off the shoulder blue taffeta dress with short puffy sleeves and a fitted bodice falling into a V shaped waistline. The skirt flared out to a mid-calf length and the folds of fabric gathered at the hemline puffing out all the way around. One look and I was sold. Martha agreed.

With the dress selected, next came an elbow length veil with a spray of lace and pearls curving down the side of my face ending at the jaw line. Perfect. No need to look any further.

After riding the best wedding dress wave for a couple weeks, Mom called.

"Linda. I can't find a flight to come to Florida," she said. "It's a holiday weekend you know. The Monday after is President's Day."

What I wanted to reply was something along the lines of, "What do you want me to do, change the date?" I had learned over the years to filter my thoughts away from being formed on my lips when it came to my mother.

"Mom. You live in New York and this is Florida in the winter. There has to be a flight you can get on." I tried hard not to voice my frustration.

"There isn't," she insisted.

"Call a different travel agent. Try a different airline," I replied.

"Don't patronize me," she said. Using the word patronize was another of her favorite phrases to toss out when she didn't get her own way.

"Mom. I can't help you. I've got enough to do getting everything ready."

She finally agreed to try again without asking about any of the other wedding plans, showing no interest in me and my big day. A pattern familiar to me and I expected nothing less.

Six weeks later the bridal salon called saying my dress arrived. I set an appointment for the fitting, put the phone down and sighed a deep sigh of remorse. My traditional side said my mother should participate in this event. She lived in New York City so I wasn't going to ask and besides, I didn't feel like listening to her go on and on about how she wished she was the one getting married because I knew she'd twist it around to make it about her sad life. Plus I didn't want to hear about the shortage of airplanes flying along the eastern seaboard.

My rebellious side said I could do this by myself. The knot in my heart told me I didn't want to do this alone. I called June.

Sitting in the chair in the dressing room at the bridal store turned out to be a thrill for June. She never expected such an honor, only glad to be a guest at the affair and nothing more. The saleswoman gingerly unwrapped the dress and helped me to slip it over my head. She clipped the veil onto my hair.

"You look um, you look like a bride!" June exclaimed, holding one of her famous tissues to her eye, dabbing the tears.

All I needed was that small confirmation that I mattered. Most of my life, I searched for that love of family. I'd fallen in love with Richard and together we would be a strong, supportive couple, but I wanted to surround us with the love of others. June stood in where my biological family could not and we both relished in the mother daughter tradition of the fitting of the wedding dress.

The wedding went off without a hitch. Mom arrived in time for all the festivities. I left her in the hands of my sisters who fixed her dress with a bad case of static cling and combed her hair so she didn't look like she'd just gotten out of bed.

June showed up in her bargain designer dress, wore the orchid corsage I selected for her, and graciously deferred to Mom as the mother of the bride. Dad walked me down the aisle and remembered his line as I rehearsed him. I twisted the traditional response to include everyone important to me.

"Who gives this woman to this man?" the judge asked.

"Her family does," he answered.

"Last week the candle factory burned down. Everyone just stood around and sang Happy Birthday." -Stephen Wright (Comedian, not my brother)

CHAPTER TWENTY-ONE

One of the good things about having Dad and June close by was the family dinners we had together, something I never had while I was growing up. My father worked and hadn't been around much. My grandparents, aunts, uncles and cousins all lived in Michigan and only made occasional visits to Cleveland. We had a lot of practice on how not to act as a family unit, a trait that has followed me into my adult life for better or worse.

June called and invited Richard and me over for Sunday dinner to celebrate my birthday. Richard liked her cooking and so did my father so that's all that mattered. She made all the effort to glue us back together.

I drove over around 4 pm. Richard would come after work. He sold furniture so the weekends were his best commission earning days. When I walked in the front door June immediately handed me a glass of white wine. The usual plate of fancy cheese and crackers waited on the coffee table in the living room.

Being the youngest, no one in my family ever made a fuss over my birthday. Mom would take me to the grocery store and let me pick out what I wanted for dinner. I picked shrimp or scallops or some kind of fish. Martha, to this day, won't eat fish yet she gave birth to a son, Scott, whose favorite meal is boiled Maine lobster. Genes manifest themselves in unusual ways.

I never had a birthday party, you know the kind where your invite your friends over, they bring presents, or spend the night in sleeping bags on the floor in the basement. Being the youngest, no one had energy left to pay attention to a birthday that wasn't in April.

April meant lots of birthday cake and ice cream in our house. Mom's birthday was on the 9th, Susan, the 16th, Grandma Husen, the 17th and Martha on the 18th. Presents and cards could be bought in bulk, never leaving anyone out. Being in a houseful of Aries, meant they were all hardheaded and jockeying for control. Being the quiet, shy and gentle Virgo, I was easy to ignore with all those big egos dancing around. When the power struggles heated up, I slunk back into the corner and read a Nancy Drew mystery.

When my birthday rolled around at the end of August, Mom's energy focused on getting all four children back to school with new shoes, a coat, sweaters and dresses. Pants for Steve, but shopping for them took far less time than finding a new outfit for two teenagers and a kindergartner. Planning a party with invitations, hats and a pin the tail on the donkey was too exhausting. I had to settle for a seafood dinner I loved with a family who hated fish and that made us all miserable.

Richard always makes a big fuss over my special day with lots of fanfare and presents big and small all individually wrapped. Even the scratch off lottery tickets we liked to exchange came wrapped in pretty paper tied with a ribbon. But I received only an occasional birthday card from the rest of my family over the years. Susan typically sent one in July, mailing my card and Steve's at the same time. He got his on time and I got mine a month early. See what I mean about conserving their energy?

June, however never forgot the day. Which also meant Dad didn't forget my birthday either while June was in charge. She deferred to Dad when it came to birthdays and holidays, reminding him of the days and picking out the cards, letting us all believe he remembered. Once she allowed him to purchase our Christmas gifts. He bought four of the most awful looking cookie jars on the planet. Mine was a huge yellow cat with painted on whiskers. I don't even like cats. Susan, who loves cats probably got the dog. Since he lived nearby to me I had to leave the monstrosity on my kitchen counter for a couple years. My siblings, living a thousand mile away, probably took theirs to the Goodwill as soon as the snow thawed.

It wasn't until Dad died that I realized June loved to have a reason to celebrate. She liked to shop and pick out small gifts for me. As she got older it was easier for her to give gift cards to the bookstore, which I never grew tired of. She never forgot me and my love of books.

Shana stood next to me on the sofa. I kept one hand on my wine glass and one hand on her back, gently stroking her black, curly poodle hair, back and forth in a steady tempo. She wouldn't leave my side.

"I taught Shana a new trick. Want to see it?" Dad rose from his favorite chair and stepped to the middle of the living room.

"Sure," I replied.

"Shana. Come," he ordered. She left the comfort of my warm, soothing hand before sitting obediently at his feet to stare intently into her master's eyes.

Dad looked down at Shana. Shana looked up at him. He pointed his index finger, raised his thumb and curled his other fingers in to form the shape of a gun.

"Shana. Would you rather be married or dead?" he asked while pointing his gun toting hand.

Shana lay down, rolled over on her back and became motionless. Dad broke out in a huge smile and I laughed. He must have spent hours getting this large fancy dog to rollover and play dead at his command. June busied herself in the kitchen ignoring the dog trick show which I'm sure she'd heard a million times. When Richard arrived, Dad put Shana through her paces once again. We laughed some more.

June refused my help in the kitchen as usual and put dinner on the table by herself. Pot roast on all her finest china laid spread out on the dining room table.

My father loved pot roast. I hated pot roast.

Growing up, pot roast was about the only meal my mother ever cooked. My father loved it, she knew how to make it and us kids suffered through it, not being allowed to leave the table until we had cleaned out plates. We couldn't let those starving children in China get the better of us.

June never gave a second thought to what she served for dinner on my birthday. She asked Dad what they should have for Linda's birthday dinner and he answered 'pot roast'. He never thought about what the rest of us wanted. June, only wanting to please him, never thought about it either. The children hovered on the fringes of their relationship, never being allowed inside or to come between them.

Halfway through dinner Dad asked where Shana was. Usually she made her way around the dinner table begging for scraps. We were instructed not to give her any while we watched Dad sneak tidbits under the table when he thought we weren't looking.

June cleared two bowls from the table and went to the kitchen. Richard grabbed some dirty dishes and followed her.

"Oh!" We heard a squeal. "Shana. No."

Richard's cackling could be heard in the dining room.

"What's the matter?" Dad called out.

"She ate the frosting off the side of the cake," June answered.

Since it was my cake, I went to see the damage. At the edge of the small breakfast table perched the Publix cake with blue butter cream roses and 'Happy Birthday Linda' written across the top. Several pink and green birthday cake candles had been pressed into the top. Yellow cake shone through the side closest to the edge of the table, all its pretty trim and flowers missing. Shana licked her chops and cocked her head to one side, wondering what all the commotion was about.

"She did not," my father said loud enough to all of us to hear.

"Did you enjoy it Shana?" Richard said to her while rubbing her behind one ear.

"She certainly did. Come and look," I said.

"Go sit down," June rushed me out of the kitchen.

Richard returned to the table unable to stop chuckling and Dad denied his precious poodle would ever do something wrong.

I heard the strike of the match. June began to sing and Dad and Richard joined in. June set the cake in front of me. A third of it was missing. She had cut off the side Shana had eaten and served the rest, candles included.

I made a wish and blew them out while staring at the lopsided cake trying to figure out how to cut it into even slices. Finally I carved out some part square, part triangular pieces of cake. They weren't pretty but June stood by to scoop the ice cream on top in an effort to smooth things over.

Dad slipped Shana some more butter cream frosting and I pretended not to see. The older I got the harder it was for me to keep quiet about how whatever Dad said was set in stone and June went along with a smile. Especially on a day that was supposed to belong to me.

"Accept what is, let go of what was and have faith in what will be."

CHAPTER TWENTY-TWO

Christmas 1990

My Dearest "One and Only",

My present to you this year is different!

For the next 365 days, you will receive a note saying "I love you because _____."

For today, I'll begin by saying "I love you because you are a living example for the kind of person God wants us to be - perfect!"

I love you completely,

Junie

P.S. Shana says she feels the same way.

The call came from June on Christmas Day.

"Your father's in the Boca Raton hospital," she said, her voice trembling.

"What happened?" I swallowed a breath and forced the words into the receiver.

"He had a tremendous pain in his stomach. The neighbors took us to the emergency room." June sounded scared and so was I.

My insides clenched into a ball. Five years ago, Dad had an aortic aneurysm repaired. At the time, they'd lived in Tampa. I flew there and drove June in Dad's big Cadillac, back and forth to the hospital every day. June never learned how to drive and I had never driven a tank before but she turned the keys over to me anyway.

The doctor discovered the aneurysm during a routine physical. Dad visited his doctor religiously and took pretty good care of himself. He was more sedentary than he should have been since he retired, but he did walk Shana several times a day. The surgery successful, he got back to living a happy life for the next five years. Now this.

I rushed to the hospital, which was about five miles away. June sat in a chair next to him, holding his hand. Dad looked pale and uncomfortable in the hospital bed.

"Hey, how are you?" I tried to sound cheerful but the sight of my father in a too small blue hospital gown barely able to cover his body, tubes dripping a clear liquid into his vein, and a plastic male urinal on his bedside table made me swallow hard. I didn't need him to worry about anything other than himself but containing my own emotions wouldn't be easy.

"I've had better days, Linny." He eeked out a tiny smile.

He dozed on and off while June and I whispered so not to wake him. She told me she called the neighbors, not an ambulance to drive him to the emergency room. If June didn't believe he was in danger of dying by dialing 911, then I shouldn't worry either. To me though, Dad didn't look good. This was more serious than June let on.

"Let's see what the doctor says before we call anyone. Okay?" she said.

An hour or so later, the doctor came in. I introduced myself. He explained Dad's aortic aneurysm repair was leaking. The surgery to fix it previously had suddenly failed. He assured us it could be corrected in a typical noncommittal tone of voice doctors often use, but it couldn't be done at this hospital. They didn't have a qualified surgeon to do the operation. My father would be transferred by ambulance to Jackson Memorial Hospital in Miami. June and I should go home and pack a suitcase.

The color drained from June's face.

"Take Shana to Nancy and Doug's. They'll take care of her, Junie," my father's voice quivered as he spoke. He knew instinctively what June was thinking. Nancy and Doug were neighbors who loved Shana too. She often had play dates at their home even though they had no dogs of their own.

"Or she can come to my house," I added.

"Nancy and Doug will take her," Dad spoke emphatically this time.

Even in this time of need, the baby of the family was being instructed to bear all the responsibility but make no decisions. I took his hand, kissed him on the forehead. "We'll see you in Miami."

I dropped June off at her home and said I'd be back in an hour. At my home, Richard, his mother, Floss and her friend from Pennsylvania, Dr. Mash sat in the living room, in the glow of the Christmas lights, sipping cocktails. Richard loved cooking for holidays. Usually I was the optimistic one and Richard saw the glass as half empty, today his optimism boosted me up. While I was gone he had the table set including three places, one for Dad, June and me. Dad and June's vodka sat on the bar next to the ice bucket and the liver pate she'd made, frozen and given to me last week waited on the cocktail table surrounded by crackers.

Oh, how I wished I could join them. I loved Christmas, the sights, the sounds, and the smells. Even though Richard had a turkey in the oven, the usual comforting aroma did nothing for me. I told them I was headed to Miami. Dr. Mash offered little consolation even after putting a friendly and less professional spin from his medical perspective. I packed and left them to enjoy the holiday cheer.

Richard and Floss knew and loved Paul. He had a big, jovial, commanding way about him. He'd be fine and they knew it. This was a normal little bump in the road of life. I packed some clothes and a nightgown, kissed Richard goodbye and wished everyone a Merry Christmas.

By the time we arrived at Jackson Memorial, Dad was safely tucked in his bed in the intensive care unit. Nurses whizzed about fussing over him. He told them June and I were coming so they had placed a chair on either side of the bed for us and kept a watchful eye as well as their distance once we sat down.

"They're going to operate tomorrow morning," Dad said. "The doctor was here earlier. Seems like a nice fellow."

"Shana is at Nancy and Doug's," June said.

"I told you they wouldn't mind taking her. She likes them," he answered.

"How was the ambulance ride? They got you here pretty fast," I said trying to make conversation with a sick man not knowing what might be appropriate to divert his thoughts from tomorrow's surgery. I'd been with him in Tampa the first time he had surgery for his aneurysm, navigating hospital waiting rooms and intensive care units. He was seriously ill but he'd get through it this time too. I had to believe that.

I held his left hand and June his right. He winced and then spoke,

"Linny, take care of my Junie for me." His eyes closed and his head fell back on the pillow.

One of the nurses interrupted before I could answer. Another rushed over and began checking one of the many beeping machines Dad was connected to.

"You must leave now," Janet, one of the nurses, announced. "Visiting hours are over."

I squeezed his hand. "We'll be back in the morning."

"You can come back at 8:30," Janet said. 'Where are you staying?"

"Across the street at the Days Inn," I answered.

The Days Inn was an old, tired hotel that had seen more than its share of families tense with fear of the unknown. The one and only lamp in between the two beds tried desperately to illuminate the room. What we couldn't see wouldn't bother us, like stains on the worn beige shag carpet or holes in the faded olive green bedspreads. Neither one of us would sleep much that night anyway so that we weren't at the Ritz Carlton was a minor inconvenience.

Visiting hours didn't start until ten a.m., even though Janet, the nurse, gave us a pass to come in before the rest of the visiting crowds. June and I were both up and ready to go much earlier. This hospital was a busy, inner city, teaching hospital so we'd have to get in line at the door with the rest of the visitors wanting early admission.

We slid into the blue vinyl booth in the hotel diner. June stared at the menu. When the waiter who was also the cook came out from behind the counter to take our order she said, "Toast. And black coffee."

"That's it?" he asked.

"Do you have some cream cheese?"

"Certainly, madam."

June nibbled on the dry toast and sipped her black coffee. I loaded my coffee with cream until it became a perfect light tan color. I never could understand how she could drink it pitch black without anything lightening it up. As I took a bite of my scrambled eggs the front desk clerk came rushing through the door and stopped at our table.

"Mrs. Wright?"

"Yes," June answered. She dropped the slice of toast and her body stiffened.

"The hospital called. They need you to call them back right away." She slid a piece of paper across the table in June's direction. "Here's the number."

In the days before cell phones, we relied on pay phones and written messages. June grabbed her purse and headed to the elevator without saying a word. I left ten dollars on the table. When I caught up with her, she was in the room dialing the phone.

Dad had been rushed into surgery. We were to come to the hospital right away.

When we arrived, the large lobby already bustled with visitors. I checked us in with the receptionist. We were told to wait in a seating area near the elevators. Not speaking a word, I watched the color inch out of June's face with each passing moment we waited not knowing what was happening with Dad. After what seemed like hours, I got the word we could now go to the ICU on the fourth floor.

Janet, the kind nurse from yesterday, greeted us as the elevator doors opened. She escorted us to a small waiting room with pink walls and pink chairs. Someone had taken great care to fan out an array of old, wrinkled magazines on a wobbly coffee table in front of a maroon tweed love seat with perfect circular body impressions on the seat cushions.

"Dr. Simon will be up to see you in a few minutes." With that she left us to wait.

What is the definition of waiting? To stay where one is or delay action until a particular time or something else happens. We were in the "until something else happens" category. What that would be, neither June nor I could possibly know. The manmade commodity called time, ticked away ever so slowly.

Soon the doctor appeared in the doorway, neat and clean in a freshly pressed white coat. He had a shiny complexion with a hint of a smile. After years of delivering bad news, he'd most likely perfected his facial expression so not to cause alarm at his arrival. He shook my hand and instantly I felt a striking warmth and sincerity about him. He held my hand, not too long, just long enough; he smiled not so big as to appear happy and not too small to seem forced. Even the tone of his voice, calm yet firm struck the perfect balance for a tense situation.

I doubt I understood a single word though, as he explained the operation my father would undergo. June sat up in her chair and seemed to be following each word he said, but June had a long history acting as if she was interested but really wasn't. She scribbled an unrecognizable signature on the surgery permission document.

The doctor disappeared and we were left to wait once again.

I slipped a year old People magazine out of the display on the table. According to them Sean Connery was the sexiest man alive. I didn't disagree then and I still don't. He's suave and debonair even today. Besides who doesn't love James Bond? He's the coolest and always will be no matter which new actor is playing the part. I stared at the pictures, but the captions appeared foggy, my eyes unable to transmit them to my brain.

My mind wouldn't focus on the words on the page. I flipped through the magazine stopping to look at some ads. June twisted the tissue she kept tucked up her sleeve. The magazines held no interest for her today either. So we sat and waited without speaking a single word, which was unusual for us. When together June and I talked about everything and everybody who crossed out minds. The silence hung thick and heavy between us.

After what seemed like an hour, we began a conversation with another woman who had settled in on the opposite side of the room. Her pleasant voice began to calm us until she started to tell us all about her brother in the burn unit, and all the gory details that went along with a six month long hospital stay. I didn't want to think about what lay ahead for Dad. He too, could be facing a long hospital stay and rehabilitation. June and I may be exchanging places with woman who longed for relief from her days inside a burn unit. Only time would tell.

A tall young man with a head full of thick dark curls entered the room. He wore green hospital scrubs and white sneakers.

"Mrs. Wright?"

June half-heartedly waved her hand.

"I'm Dr. Weinberg. I'm assisting Dr. Simon with Mr. Wright's surgery." He sat down on the rickety table in front of us. I held my breath.

He extended his hand. I shook it while bracing myself for what was to come. Cold and tense.

"We had to clamp off the arteries to both his legs for an extended period of time. Before we can proceed, I need your permission to amputate both legs."

June's eyes opened wide with horror and filled with tears. My stomach knotted. The doctor waited for a reply.

"What will happen if you don't amputate?" I asked.

He wrung his hands, looked down at the floor. I suspected he was an intern sent to get a lesson in bedside manners. Not that I believe a doctor every really becomes comfortable talking to patients during these types of events, but they learn some level of relaxed demeanor in order not to escalate the level of anxiety in the patient's loved ones. Dr. Weinberg hadn't yet perfected delivering bad news to strangers.

"We will continue to try to repair the aneurysm but the blood supply has been cut off for so long, the outcome is not looking good at this point."

I turned to June. "What do you want to do?"

"You decide. His children should decide," she blotted her eyes with the now damp and shredded Kleenex. "Whatever you think is best, Linda"

That June would defer such a decision shocked me. As Dad's children we were never consulted about anything between them. Dad and June were a tight knit unit and his children never came in between them. I didn't know and never thought to ask if she'd called Susan, Martha or Steve. They lived in Ohio and Michigan and being that it's Christmas would not be able to get here quickly or easily.

Here I am, the only one of his four children available to make any kind of decision with regard to my father. My sense of urgency told me the doctor needed an answer now. He couldn't wait for me to go downstairs to the lobby and use the bank of pay phones to make three separate phone calls to my sisters and brother. My thoughts raced around my mind in a jumbled mess.

Although I didn't realize it at the time, June asked me to play God. Why? What was she afraid of? I pictured my father without legs. He loved walking his dog and taking a nap on the sofa every afternoon. His hearty laugh and infectious smile would turn sour. Was that how he would want to be? The rest of his life lay in my hands. This was not a job I wanted to have since God and I hadn't spent much time together lately. It was a choice I'd been told through the years I was incapable of making. I wondered if they'd decided together to let Linny take the reins, not to involve the rest of the kids and take the guilt off Junie's shoulders.

I turned to June hoping she'd give me a sign, anything that she agreed with me. The last thing I wanted was to cause a rift between us. She, more than I, was headed into the unknown. Our lives were about to change with the next words I spoke.

"Don't amputate. He wouldn't want to be confined to a wheel-chair," I said.

The words slid off my tongue, no getting them back now. It was done. June didn't flinch.

"Do you agree Mrs. Wright?" the doctor asked.

"Yes," she whispered. "We said our goodbyes yesterday."

He got up quickly and raced out of the waiting room.

I gulped in a big breath and went back to waiting. June did the same. It was our only option. The decision I made careened around my brain and hung heavy on my heart. I waited for it to crash and stop even for a second, so I could look at it, examine it, make sure it was the right decision. It was too late. I had already tossed my words out into the universe.

We didn't wait long before the nervous intern returned. I could see in his face what he was about to say.

"He's gone. I'm sorry."

June let out a yelp, turned and threw her arms around me. Her forehead lay on my shoulder. She sobbed. As I held her, I thanked the doctor for all his help. All I could do was hold her, something I'd never done before. In the blink of an eye we moved from an arm's length relationship with Dad firmly planted in the middle to one with only the two of us for support. She lost the love of her life that day. He was only seventy-one years old and by all accounts, he left us before he was finished living. The universe moved at a fast pace.

After what seemed like an hour but probably only ten or fifteen minutes, Dr. Simon appeared, offered his condolences and asked us to follow him. The death certificate needed to be signed. He chatted without hesitation as June and I followed him up a flight of stairs, down a long, white, antiseptic hallway, around a corner and into an elevator.

"I can never remember how to get to this place," he admitted.

June and I didn't mind the walk. It felt good to move, be mindless if even for a few minutes. We took the elevator down two floors, made a right and a couple lefts through a series of confusing turns.

"OK. Here we are." He knocked on a door. It opened slowly. "Miss Alice will take good care of you."

Miss Alice greeted us. The door could only open part way. Something blocked it from being able to swing freely. I entered the room sideways sliding into a tiny square of empty floor. June came and squeezed in next to me.

I squinted in the pale light. The room had no window and one lone light bulb hanging from the center of the ceiling. Stacked to the top were old leather bound ledgers like an accountant would use, the edges of their pages rough and yellowed.

Miss Alice stood behind a metal desk and ushered us to sit in folding chairs facing her. Her voice soft was soothing, in sharp contrast to her flaming red hair piled high in an outdated beehive, and her lipstick a bright citrus orange. A wave of claustrophobia washed over me, and I chuckled at the surreal surroundings.

Miss Alice asked June to sign for my father's body. One of the musty ledgers sat open on her desk at about the halfway mark, pages piled eight inches high on each side of the book's spine. My brain had slowed down with the events of the day so when my vision adjusted to the light, I realized the books contained the name of everyone who had ever died in this hospital. I shuddered. Not exactly a history I wanted my father to be part of. Here I sat, as thousands maybe millions, based on the number of ledgers stacked up in here, of people had before me, numb, unable to process the impact of such a loss. June squeezed herself behind the desk, took the pen from Miss Alice's hand and signed on the line she pointed to with her cherry red fingernail.

I remember Miss Alice because of her love of the color red and I will never forget her for the warmth and kindness she displayed to us that day. She knew we were still in the foggy phase, still able to smile and laugh and make small talk with a stranger. She also knew that wouldn't last for long before we plunged head first into the grief phase, unable to find words without tears springing from our eyes. Miss Alice truly cared for all the loved ones of the newly deceased with whom she was charged with keeping track of and I am grateful for the memory of her to this day.

June and I walked out of the hospital doors into a cool and crisp December day even for Miami. McDonald's Golden Arches glowed in front of us.

"I need something to eat before I start making phone calls. How about you?" I asked. The energy from few bites of breakfast I had early this morning had been used up hours ago.

"I've never eaten in a McDonald's in my life." June's pale expression floated in front of me.

"Now's as good a time as any to start." We both laughed while I ordered two Big Macs, two fries and two diet cokes. We sat at a tiny white table for two with hard red chairs and ate without speaking.

June would face many firsts over the next few months. Many of those firsts were bound to bring her grief to the surface in ways she didn't want or expect. Eating a greasy cheeseburger was easy compared with what was surely yet to come. She looked like she was enjoying it.

"I guess red is the color of the day," I said before popping the last French fry in my mouth.

June let out her girlish giggle. "Miss Alice was awfully nice even though she looked like something out of a cartoon." She hadn't laughed or smiled in quite that way in days.

Christmas of 1990 was a blur of sparkling lights on decorated trees in sterile hospital wards. Presents sat under the tree, wrapped, never to be opened by their recipients. Love letters promised for 365 days would never be written. One unexpected death had the power to change the course of many lives forever.

"The struggle you're in today is developing the strength you need for tomorrow." – Anonymous

CHAPTER TWENTY-THREE

Looking back to those months after Dad's funeral, my life went on as usual. I started a new job, passed the CPA exam and soon moved into a brand new home of my dreams. June, however, worked very hard at making sure everyone believed her life had remained exactly the same and she didn't need help especially from me.

If June found herself bursting into tears when Dad's death certificate arrived in the mail or when she found a bottle of his cologne tucked into a drawer she missed after cleaning out his things, or even setting the dinner table for only one, I'll never know. Every time I offered to take her out to dinner or shopping, both things she loved to do, she put on a good front; she was doing just fine. I could see no cracks in the facade, nor did I take the time to look any deeper for them. I had to live my own life.

Nancy and Doug, the neighbors who had so graciously taken Shana in, stepped up and offered to drive June to the grocery store and hairdresser appointments. Doug bought a big, brand new boat like Cadillac every two years and had no problem giving Shana the same leather passenger seat my father had allowed her in his own car. Minimizing the disruption in the dog's life seemed the most important thing June could do for herself.

They fell into a routine and every Saturday when I called to see how June was doing, she relayed some antic of Shana's and some dumb remark of Doug's. I never thought Nancy and Doug were the kind of people June would call friends. June loved the big city, they appeared small townish. Doug was a big, overweight, lumbering kind of guy, who wore a long, expressionless face no matter what his mood. Nancy, on the other hand, wore the pants in the family, stern, precise, never missing a single detail.

Because they were so kind to June, Richard and I often included them in our dinner parties. Doug loved being around my friends who were younger and livelier. He had an eye for the girls, and was a tad on the dirty old man side. He loved to socialize and tell silly jokes, while Nancy stewed in the corner.

The cracks began to appear slowly but surely. First Shana, at the age of eleven, had to be put down. The loss of a family pet is never easy and June dragged it out spending all of her available dollars at the veterinarian in a grand effort to keep Shana alive and vibrant. Based on Shana's age and size, it was her time, but June struggled to let her go because it also meant the grieving process for her beloved Paul was about to start all over again.

Without Shana to act as a buffer between June and Nancy and Doug, Nancy boldly announced they would no longer be available to drive June wherever she needed to go. June told me that she accommodated their schedule when making her appointments but I suspect they grew tired of being at her beck and call. Nancy and Doug loved Shana but possibly June showed her stubborn and controlling side too often to suit their simple lifestyle. According to June, she also added this;

"Linda only invited us over so we would bring you too."

This statement is sort of true I will admit. They did make my life easier by not driving 6 miles one way from my house to pick up June and to take her back home at the end of the night after I downed several glasses of wine.

I like to think I welcomed all kinds of people into my home, for the sheer pleasure it gave me to share what Richard and I had to give. Nancy and Doug blessed my family in our time of need and I'm thankful for them. It made me sad she pulled the plug without any notice and without allowing me to explain myself.

I should have paid attention to this blip in the road because I would run into it again later when June thought she made all the necessary arrangements to care for herself. She believed she had not a worry in the world; her friends would look after her well-being. What she never considered is they believed the responsibility for June belonged to me. I wish Dad had given me a little more insight through the years into how June's mind worked before he burdened me with his final words. He knew what he was asking me to do without giving me the tools I needed to do it.

* * *

"Linda, it's time for me to move closer to you. In Delray, into a smaller place," June announced shortly after Nancy made her proclamation. "I talked with a real estate agent and she's lining up some places for me to see tomorrow. I put this house up for sale yesterday."

"Great idea, June." I said. "It'll be more fun to have you closer. Richard and I will look around here too and give you a heads up if anything looks interesting."

"I don't really want to leave my Boca Raton address but after that hurricane, I don't want to be alone here any longer."

Hurricane Andrew ran through Miami like a buzz saw on Sunday, August 24, 1992, approximately a year and half after Dad died. As always June had planned a Sunday dinner since my birthday fell during the week that year. We had to cancel when the area was placed under a hurricane warning and we were ordered to hunker down. I invited June to spend the night at our new, three bedroom, solidly built, concrete block house, but she refused. That stubborn streak of hers popped up at the strangest times and always when all I wanted to do was help and be kind to her.

The category five storm barreled through south Miami, devastating everything in its path. In Palm Beach County, 75 miles north of Andrew's landfall, we suffered minimal wind damage. Hurricanes for some reason seem to come through at night, in the pitch dark making them even more menacing.

"I spent the night in the downstairs powder room and I never want to do that again," June told me. Her voice sounded raw and crackly like she spent the night hollering for help.

"Why did you do that?" I asked, dumfounded that she felt the need to cram herself into a bathroom the size of a postage stamp with only room for a toilet and a sink, barely enough space to sit down when she could have spent the night sleeping in my comfortable guest room.

"It's the only room in the house without a window. That's where they told me to go," she said.

"Who told you to go there?" I asked, thinking one of her worry-wart neighbors thought they were doing her a favor but instead struck fear in her mind.

"On the news, they said to take shelter. Didn't you?" she asked. I sensed frustration in her voice.

"No, June," I said. "We went to bed and slept through it. The storm was a hundred miles away from us. We had some wind and very little rain."

"Don't patronize me, Linda. I don't like your tone." She used that word my mother loved to say. The hair on my arms bristled.

"June, I asked you to come over but you refused. Nothing happened here and you spent the night worrying over nothing. All you had to do was call me."

Click went the phone. Within three months time, June settled into a perfect two bedroom condominium only a quarter mile from my home. The apartment had two spacious bathrooms, an eat-in kitchen and a lovely balcony where she could smoke to her heart's content. It had one other important thing. Hurricane shutters and a handyman willing to close them for a small fee.

A Bittersweet Goodnight

"It's not denial. I'm just selective about the reality I accept." – Anonymous

CHAPTER TWENTY-FOUR

"Hey, June. Wanna go out for dinner on Saturday night?" I asked. "Richard's working late."

"I never say no to going out for dinner," she answered.

"Do you want to try Ruby Tuesday's over in Mizner Park? Something other than Outback for a change?" I asked.

"Sure. I'm game," June said.

"Okay. I'll pick you up at five."

We made these dates for dinner every few weeks. Girls only. If Richard worked late, June and I would go out for dinner and more than a few drinks. I found our dates to be fun and a happy diversion from the monotony of drinking at home. I loved my wine but wasn't one to sit alone at a bar drinking while Richard worked. I'm sure June felt the same way.

June loved Outback and the two for one happy hour. I liked spending time with her, we'd chatter and drink and eat and chatter some more. I respected the person June was in my life and it was never a chore to make sure she was properly entertained.

Being we were in Boca Raton, Florida in March during what we refer to as 'season' when our shops and eateries are filled with Northerners escaping the cold winter, we arrived at the restaurant at 5:15 pm, there was already a long wait. I put my name on the list and got a pager in return. I found an empty bench outside across from the park where we could people watch, a pastime we found we had in common all those years ago at the racetrack.

When together June and I never ran out of trivial things to talk about. We weren't ever going to solve the problems of the world or comment on the state of politics in this country. We had plenty of insignificant items to discuss, like whether June would like to read the Harry Potter books, what that stain really was on Monica Lewinsky's dress or try to agree on the last time it actually rained.

There was one question June never failed to ask me when we were together. I guess she viewed it as the kind of thing needed to break the ice. I never thought we needed any kind of conversation starter but she asked anyway.

"What do you hear from Susan or Steve?" June asked.

"June. You know they never call me. They don't even send me an email," I said. "I don't know what's going on with them.

I'm not close with my siblings. Periodically we may exchange an email or a text. These days I mainly learn what's going on in their lives and those of their children on Facebook. When I click the like button they know I've seen their latest adventures. That seems to be enough for us. Back then being I was the sibling living furthest away from the others, I stayed in the dark about their comings and goings. I longed for more personal relationships from my family but I still hadn't learned that family means a wide variety and levels of interactions.

"I don't hear anything from them either," she said.

The sad part was, I was used to being kept on the fringes, but here I sat next to an old woman who waited for little tidbits of news or photos from children she'd known for over forty years. Through me she hoped she get some tiny fragment of daily life that she could share with the neighbors to make her feel loved and important. It never happened.

"What's Richard up to these days?" To ask me about my husband was the next best thing. He loved getting into mischief so I must be able to tell her some kind of funny story she could pass along to the other gossiping old ladies she hung around with.

"I'm so mad at him," I answered. "He's got his pants all in a wad about something stupid. I asked him to take my car to the dealership to look at the tires while I was away in California for work and you'd think I was asking him to give me a million dollars."

"What do you say to him when you're mad at him?" June asked. "I can't picture you two having a fight."

"We can fight like cats and dogs." I didn't want to reveal more than that to June about my marriage. Like any marriage, Richard and I had our ups and downs and I kept the downs to myself. I didn't share the details with anyone, and especially not June.

"If I'm only a little bit annoyed with him, I'll call him a jerk," I said. "And if I'm mad, I'll call him an asshole."

"So how mad are you at him right now?" June asked with a wicked smirk on her face.

"Right now I'm calling him a really nasty bleeping kind of asshole."

June held her hand over her mouth and giggled as she always did. She rested her chin on her chest, scrunched up her nose and snickered like a little girl.

The pager in my hand started to vibrate.

Once seated, the first thing we did before looking at the menu was to order drinks. If it was happy hour we got two at once. For me two glasses of house white wine. I had no reason to spend my money on more expensive wine, I gulped it down so fast I couldn't taste the difference between cheap and expensive.

June used to say to the waiter, "Bring me whatever kind of vodka. It doesn't matter."

Even though she insisted on paying the bill during our dinner outings, I told her to stop saying that.

"They bring you the most expensive vodka they have," I explained to her.

"I don't need that," she said leaning back into the booth shocked anyone would take advantage of her in that way. "I can't tell the difference. I water it down with ice."

"I know. So say the well liquor is what you want. It's cheaper," I instructed.

We both finished one drink before our food came and when the waitress delivered our hamburgers and fries, we each ordered another two drinks before happy hour ended. I had a habit of pushing the empty wine glasses to the edge of the table so a passing server would pick them up on their way to the kitchen. I didn't want anyone to start counting or stop serving me.

June and I never stopped talking over our favorite alcohol and fat juicy burger. Was it the alcohol the made our tongues wag over the nonsense we loved to laugh about? Or did we enjoy each other's company because of the alcohol? Would our relationship be what it is if it didn't include the temptation? I'd say a combination of all of the above.

About three bites into our hamburger, June set hers down on the plate.

"You know Linda, your father and I never had a fight," she said. "Not in all the years we were married."

"Never?" I asked knowing I had witnessed a doozy of an argument over the racetrack years ago.

"We always agreed," she said.

"Did you always defer to him so there wouldn't be a fight?" I asked with a devilish tone in my voice. Without the wine, I wouldn't have been bold enough to ask this question.

"I didn't have to. I don't think we ever disagreed." June took another drink of her water-downed vodka.

If June hadn't been drinking would she answer that way? Denying what she knew wasn't true, she stuffed the truth into a dark spot where she didn't see it so she could keep the myth of her marriage alive.

Today, as a recovering alcoholic, I regret the chances I took, drinking and driving and then depositing a drunk old woman at the door to her condominium hoping she made it up the elevator and down the hall to her apartment without injury. I wonder if food and drink was the glue holding us together or if it was the dividing line between truth and fiction.

"The expected is what keeps us steady. It's the unexpected that changes our lives forever."
— Shonda Rhimes

CHAPTER TWENTY-FIVE

I'm not sure which niece's birthday we were celebrating. If it was Alex, then it would have been the beginning of November, a pleasant time of year in Florida with warm days and cool evenings. If it was Lauren's then it would have been the beginning of April, also an enjoyable time outside between seasons in Florida.

Steve's wife, Karen had come for a visit with the two girls and her mother, Diane. All four of them stayed in June's crowded apartment. Even though she invited them to stay with her, the minute they left, she ranted and raved over how miserable and exhausted she was. June was approaching eighty years old and no longer had all the energy she used to.

June gave them her bed and slept on the couch during their visits. The little girls would have been perfectly happy sleeping on the living room floor, like having a slumber party. June wouldn't allow it. She was in a tizzy for weeks before their arrival trying to plan the meals and map out activities for them. All of which were unnecessary since Karen made their vacation agenda long before ever stepping foot on the airplane. I tried to explain this to June but she would have none of it. In her mind, they were her guests not mine and she would decide. Her stubborn streak appeared just in time to interrupt a fun family time.

"You know I have to set the rules while they're here," June told me on our Saturday grocery store run.

"What are the rules?" I asked.

"No jumping in the elevator. The girls always want to do that, you know," she said.

"What's wrong with that? Richard does it all the time," I asked.

June's face turned red, her expression soured. "They'll break the elevator. I won't allow them to do it." Mostly June loved Richard but she hated it when he undermined her well thought out plans. He made mischief every chance he could and she wanted things to go her way and in her poorly thought out order.

I knew better than to say the elevator would remain operational if two seventy-pound children jumped up and down a few times. She'd never speak to me again. The rest of the rules covered meal times, bed times and use of the television remote control. Did she know these people were coming to vacation?

To give June some relief, I invited everyone over to celebrate the birthday. Richard and I planned to grill steaks, bake potatoes and fill the table with all the trimmings. A personalized cake with ice cream and candles to blow out would be the perfect ending. I also stopped at Wal-Mart to pick up one of those helium balloon canisters. The patio looked festive with balloons of all colors floating from our chairs.

Richard is known in our family circle as the Magic Man. He has a small repertoire of tricks to delight both young and old. After we stuffed ourselves silly with cake and ice cream, the magic show began. I took that as a cue to clear the table and clean up. I'd seen these tricks so many times over the years I could do his routine in my sleep.

The thing about his tricks are that the older the nieces got, the smarter they became.

"Uncle Richard, they're the same size," Lauren laughed when he hauled out two curved pieces of colored paper that created an optical illusion.

"How'd you get so smart?" he'd ask, deflated his secret had been figured out. "I bet you don't know how I can do this."

With that he fished a balloon out of a bag, stuck it on the nozzle of the half full helium tank filling it part way. Pinching the end, he held the balloon to his mouth and sucked in some of the gas.

"Happy birthday to you," he sang in a high, squeaky, Donald Duck kind of a voice that helium causes.

I doubled over laughing, Alex and Lauren squealed with delight and June stared wide-eyed at Richard with her mouth agape. She'd never seen or heard the helium trick before.

The girls tried it next, much to their mother's consternation. Alex laughed so hard she couldn't form words. The anticipation of the squeaky voice far out did the actual speech. I held my stomach it hurt so much, full of cake and ice cream being jostled around by hysteria.

Richard filled another balloon and handed it to June. We waited while she held the balloon between her fingers trying to decide whether she should partake. Then it happened. She held the balloon to her lips and drew in a deep breath.

"Am I really going to talk funny?" she squeaked like Minnie Mouse.

I howled, Karen and Diane roared, Richard laughed, the girls giggled non-stop. June took in another breath and started talking again. Doubled over with laughter, I couldn't stand up straight.

June took in a third gulp. By this time the sound of laughter mixed with unintelligible words in the tone of a duck permeated the night. Tears rolled down our faces and June relished being the center of attention.

Had I mixed her drinks a little too strongly that night? Did she come to the realization that jumping in the elevator was harmless? Was June growing older and little by little letting her guard down and finally starting to enjoy life as part of our family?

That night she made a memory that will live in our family archives for a very long time.

*"Life can only be understood backwards;
but it must be lived forwards."
— Soren Kierkegaard*

CHAPTER TWENTY-SIX

The next letter I pulled out of the pile was addressed to me. I don't know how this letter made it into a box on June's shelf. Maybe she wrote it and never mailed it to me. When my first story was published in *Chicken Soup for the Soul*, I was ecstatic and of course mailed her an autographed copy of the book.

3/31/11

Dear Linda,

Thank you so much for sending the book of dog stories. Your article on Ginger is delightful. I really think that having a dog in your family is one of the special pleasures we can have.

Of course, there is one problem. Are you having trouble
coping with Ginger's ego now that her story has been published?
Give her a hug from me and enjoy the season.

Love,

June

In 2009 Richard and I made the most impulsive decision of our married life to move 150 miles north of Delray to a new area in Brevard County, Florida called Viera. I'd been laid off from my job of fifteen years in the corporate headquarters of Office Depot. Richard was ready to retire and we both needed a change. What we didn't anticipate however, was the Great Recession.

June didn't take the news well and refused to come with us. No amount of coaxing or bribery could change her mind. I knew she'd push back as irrational a response as she could think of. She had no one else close in her life, no children of her own, no one who took an active interest in her well being besides Richard and me.

"I won't be able to sell my apartment," she argued.

"Richard and I will buy you a condo near us. You can pay rent if that makes you feel better," I answered. "We'll cover you until your condo is sold." This might be a stretch for us financially but one we were willing to take to keep June safe. Although still in fairly good health, she was closing in on ninety years old.

"I'm not moving. You go." She stomped her foot, her stubborn ways surfaced at the news she didn't want to hear. Or when what she thought benefited her and her alone was being yanked out of her control. Moving and starting a whole new life would be scary for me too so I understand her point of view. Going it alone seemed even more frightening to me.

I've often thought about why June never learned to drive a car. She was an intelligent, independent woman and driving is part of being self-sufficient. She wanted us all to believe, my father included, she was afraid of everyone else on the road, not her own skills behind the wheel. After all these years of watching her talk people into giving her a ride wherever she needed to go, put June in control. She got the rest of us to drop our own lives and drive her around town whenever she needed to go on an errand. I built my personal schedule around June and that's exactly what June wanted me to do.

I was raised to respect the wishes of my parents and grandparents, adults in general. I'd been taught not to talk back so I didn't. If that's what she wanted, who was I to say. She took care of herself without my help, and that wouldn't change just because I wasn't nearby any longer. June threw a temper tantrum because I was no longer under her control.

The day I left for good, I went to say goodbye. I don't remember what we said to each other. I only remember hugging her as June's small, frail frame became lost in my arms. The last memory of June that day was feeling the sharpness of her bony shoulder blades sticking out through her sweater. We both quickly released our hug; I turned and walked down the corridor, anxious to drive to my new home and my new life, not having a second thought about what I was leaving behind. Except for June.

"I'll miss you," June called out. "I love you."

I stopped. June had never spoken those special three words to me before. Ever. Growing up, those words had never been tossed around by anyone in my family let alone my parents.

I turned around. As she lifted her hand to wave goodbye, she rubbed her hand against her face, hoping I wouldn't notice her tears.

"I love you too," as I waved goodbye. In my heart I felt a pang of remorse at leaving her here all alone but I didn't stop myself from walking away.

* * *

Richard and I lived in our new home for about six months. It had been a rough road, adapting to a new place and new way of life. I'd been unsuccessful in finding any kind of work. The year was 2009, the height of the great recession. Since I no longer had a regular job, I immersed myself into my passion, writing.

I read about a creative writing workshop at a local university and signed myself up. The first day of the seminar, my body tingled with excitement. I decided to take the classes in personal essays, fiction novel writing and screenplays. When I walked into my first class, one on individual stories, I didn't know if the high came from the fact that I really wanted to hone my writing skills, or that the professor standing at the front of the room welcoming his students, was one, handsome, sexy hunk of a guy.

A man in his fifties, gracefully graying, who obviously spent some time in the gym, wore a pair of broken-in jeans and a tight fitting t-shirt. I stared. This class would be even better than I imagined.

"Let's get started," he said running his fingers through a gorgeous head of hair. "Write a letter to your father."

I gulped.

The rest of the students began writing at a furious pace. I struggled to get even one word on the page. This wouldn't be easy. My guilt at leaving June was never far from my thoughts. I finally got something down before the dreamy professor called time and asked us to stop.

"Who would like to read first?" he asked. No one raised his or her hand.

He leaned in to read my nametag. "Linda, read yours to us." The brief whiff of his cologne did little to calm me even though it smelled quite delicious.

I screwed up my face as if to say, "Do I have to?"

"Go ahead. We're simply learning. None of us is passing judgment here. Those are the rules of my classroom."

I didn't want to be one of those whiny people in a class who expect to be taught something but don't want to participate in the process. I drew in a deep breath and began to read.

> *Dear Dad,*
>
> *I know you asked me to take care of June before you died. Richard and I have tried hard to do that over the years. But now we needed to do something for ourselves. She's stubborn and refused to move here with us. I know you know that side of her. We've found peace here. My hope was that June would find it here too.*

Gasping for air, I couldn't hold back the tears any longer. Like a rushing waterfall, they streamed down my face. I fished through my purse for some tissue while the other students stared.

"You didn't expect that to happen did you?" the professor asked.

"No," I managed to squeeze out. "My father died twenty years ago and he asked me to take care of his wife."

"If writing and reading don't evoke some kind of deep thought and emotion, then you've wasted your time. Good job," he said. "Who wants to go next?"

A man in the back raised his hand. His letter to his father created a scene where he saw his father eating at Burger King but didn't stop to talk to him. The crevice of time too deep. My reason for turning on the tears seemed insignificant in comparison.

My father spoke to me from some other realm that day. He let me know in a very public way all was well and Richard and I had his blessing. We had looked after June well and he considered my promise kept. If I learned nothing else from the cool and hunky writing teacher, at least I broke the ice for all the sad and tearful letters to fathers who unknowingly burdened their children with baggage too heavy to lift time and time again. I allowed them to release their pain even if only for a little while.

"Advice is what we ask for when we already know the answer but wish we didn't."
– Erica Jong

CHAPTER TWENTY-SEVEN

Rushing to get out the door for work, the phone rang. Not that I worried about being late to my part time job trying to get a real estate agent's files organized. She paid me ten dollars an hour and I spent time throwing out year old flyers. The job gave me a little pin money and got me out of the house but no long-term career path. Today something told me I should answer the phone.

"Linda. It's Rosemary. I live next door to June."

My stomach clenched into a knot. I knew very well who Rosemary was and where she lived.

"I'm going to put my neighbor, Barbara on the phone," she said.

Rosemary was also an elderly widow, but at least ten years younger than June. The two enjoyed gossiping over an evening cocktail accompanied by some cheddar cheese chunks and low salt Triscuits. At least that's what June told me.

"Hi Linda. I'm Barbara and I live down the hall," the stranger said. "June fell. We found her in her bedroom this morning."

"Is she alright?" I couldn't think of what else to say.

"She won't let us call the paramedics." She gave the phone to Rosemary.

"How is she?" I asked again.

Rosemary took in a breath. "I've never seen her so angry. She made me swear I wouldn't call you. I don't know how long she'd been there but I noticed her newspaper outside her door and it was after ten o'clock. Joe lifted her off the floor and you know Joe isn't healthy."

Each time I begged June to get the Life Alert after I moved away, she insisted she didn't need it because she and Rosemary had a pact. They each had keys to the other's apartment and if the newspaper was still outside, it should be cause for alarm. Rosemary was going to save her. That's exactly how it played out. June boohooed me every time I insisted it wasn't a reliable plan.

At some point, she gave in however, and called one day to let me know she purchased one. At the time, I thought I won. Little did I know, June was always the one in charge. She paid the bill for it each month and wore the button around her neck but nothing else.

Joe was another neighbor who June often hung out with during the day. He'd suffered a couple of heart attacks before the age of 65. His wife Darlene, worked during the day so he and June kept each other company. I know he kept his eye on her while letting her vent about how I left her but he was hardly in a position physically to lift a 95-pound woman off the floor. What kind of tragic situation had I created for June and her friends by moving away?

"Didn't she have the button around her neck?" I asked.

"She never takes it off but she won't push it," Rosemary said.

What was my job here supposed to be? June wanted to be left alone to die. I wasn't nearby any longer, but was I helping her do that or was I keeping her from doing it? The flaw in her plan however, was that her neighbors cared about her. Now they called me because they didn't want to be held responsible for watching over her.

Based on this conversation with Rosemary and the unknown and never before mentioned neighbor, neither knew they were a part of June's grand plan. She told me they were all on board in order to keep me away.

"She's okay though. She's not in any pain and she's sitting on the sofa," Rosemary said.

The conversation became muffled. "Barbara wants to talk to you again."

"I noticed there aren't as many vodka bottles in the trash lately," she said.

The trash room in the condo was down the hall. The only exercise June got was taking her trash there. Since she refused to use her walker or a cane, taking out the trash became a full-fledged outing. She tied up a garbage bag and held it in her right hand. The left hand steadied her by inching ever so slowly down the outside wall. When she reached a doorway, she stopped, planted her feet firmly, and balanced herself before taking the three of four steps needed before her hand reached the wall again.

The door to the trash room was left propped open because the other residents saw her and took mercy on her. She left her bag on the floor or dropped the vodka bottle in the recycle bin before repeating the walk home. June headed straight to the patio to smoke once that chore was completed.

"You can't tell her we called you. You must promise us," Rosemary begged.

A picture of June with a cast iron frying pan in her hand chasing Rosemary down the walkway entered my mind. What on earth were these people afraid of? How could she possibly bring any harm to them? She only wanted to be left alone to die.

Since moving either Richard or I called her every few days. Richard told her stupid jokes like "Why wouldn't the cat climb the tree?" June would think a few seconds before giving up.

Richard would say, "Because he's afraid of the bark."

The two of them would laugh and giggle like they were in the same room. I'd ask if she needed anything. Once she said she couldn't find her glasses so I put a couple pairs of cheap readers in the overnight mail. We tried as best we could to make sure she didn't fret.

I answered that question for myself. Responsibility. June must have spoken to her friends often about how I had abandoned her. They surely agreed and had no qualms about calling the nearest relative to relieve themselves of liability. The family must take care of aging members not the neighbors. They had come to her rescue this time but that was their limit. The ball had been thrown into my lap. It was now my turn to do something about her. They did the right thing by not honoring June's wish to keep a secret from me.

"I won't tell her. Don't worry I'll figure out something." I had no idea what I was going to do next, but it was clear something had to be done.

* * *

I admit I waited a day before I called June in deference to Rosemary's request. That is how totally clueless I was about how to help her. Was it selfish on my part? I'll say selfish. I have a long history of selfish. Even though I had plenty of free time, I wasn't working, had a good car to get me there, and plenty of friends in the area who would love for me to visit. I simply didn't want to go. Richard and I had found a new home and didn't want to be dragged back into the old. I really had abandoned June, like she told everyone I had. I jumped overboard into a new part of the ocean, a place she thought too difficult to navigate at this time of her life. I had the life ring ready and waiting only she couldn't see it and didn't have the energy to reach for it.

"Hi June. It's Linda." For years anytime I called I simply started talking without introducing myself. Lately I began by saying my name.

"How are you?" she answered. Her voice sounded more soft than usual with a slight tremor. Different.

"I'm good. How are you?" I said.

"I'm so confused. I don't know what I'm to do," she answered.

"What are you confused about?" I asked.

"My desk is a mess and I don't know what to do about it." I heard her breath hitch. "I think I fell. Joe came and helped me up but ever since then I've been confused."

I didn't let on I knew about the fall. I found myself under Rosemary's spell not wanting to stir up June's anger. Beside the stubbornness June also had a temper. When it was in full swing, no one wanted to be around. That went for my father too.

"How about I come down to see you and get you un-confused?" I delivered my well thought out line with ease.

"Would you do that for me?" she whimpered.

"Of course I would, June. How about I come down on Monday and I'll spend the week with you?"

"That would be nice," she murmured.

I wouldn't arrive soon enough to satisfy the neighbors but June didn't suspect I knew anything. That's the way I wanted to keep it.

After I lined up a full week for June, interviewing home aids, taking her shopping, getting her bank accounts in order and bills paid. I called her on Sunday to remind her I was coming.

"I know you're coming. Will you call me before you leave home?" she asked.

"Of course. See you tomorrow around three," I said.

"I'm looking forward to it," she replied.

I had some appointments in the morning so my plan was to leave after lunch. I packed my things in the car, kissed Richard and Ginger goodbye and drove off. With one hundred and forty miles to organize the thoughts in my head, I second guessed the arrangements I made to help June. Were they even necessary? Yesterday she sounded like herself, lucid and clear.

I know I had promised to call her when I left home but being unsure of her sense of time, I opted to wait until I reached Fort Pierce.

Fort Pierce is the halfway point to Delray. Interstate I 95 and the Florida Turnpike meet here and the exit has one fast food joint after another with a few sleazy hotels and a video sex shop sprinkled in. I pulled into Burger King.

"June. It's Linda." She picked up the phone on the first ring.

"Are you on your way?" she asked.

"Yes. I should be at your house about three thirty." I responded.

"Ok. I'll see you then. Do you have your key?"

"I do," I said, and the phone went dead.

Clouds loomed thick and gray the entire drive, adding to the feeling that two hours in the car felt more like two days. The sky spit rain as I pulled into the parking lot of the condo. Parking spaces were numbered in some kind of code. The theory being since the apartment number didn't match the parking spot number, no one would be able to figure out whose car was whose. I thought of this sarcastically as a brilliant security policy.

I felt relieved when Rosemary's red Cadillac was parked in its rightful place and not in June's space as it often was. It seems June who never owned a car or learned to drive one, owned a much more desirable parking place without the branches of a dirty oak tree hanging overhead, waiting to drop its leaves all over the unsuspecting automobile. Thunder rumbled in the distance as I pulled into parking space number 218.

A stranger held the lobby door open for me so I didn't need to buzz the apartment. The wheels of my suitcase clicked along the Chattahoochee walkway once I reached the fifth floor. The darkness of the approaching storm cast pallor across the building's catwalk. I raised my hand to knock at apartment 512 and abruptly stopped. The door was open, slightly ajar but open.

Whenever inside June threw the deadbolt and hooked the chain no matter what time of day or the number of minutes before she intended to leave again. The door was never left unlocked let alone open, no matter what.

"June?" I yelled before pushing the door open. "June?"

The blinds across the sliding glass doors at the far end of the room were drawn. No lights were turned on. My eyes struggled to adjust to the afternoon darkness. I could barely make out her small figure walking across the living room toward the bedroom. She didn't answer me. Still wearing her nightgown, I sensed something terribly wrong.

"June. What's going on?" Why aren't you dressed?"

"You made good time, didn't you?" She stood at the end of the hallway blocking my view of the living room.

"I did. What's the matter?" I asked.

The skin on her face drooped like old damask draperies hung long ago to frame a sagging window. The ravages of sun and cigarette smoke settled in and made themselves at home invading every crack and crevice. She wore none of her usual gobs of liquid makeup in a shade just a tad too orange leaving a demarcation line between the jawbone and her pale neck. Her usual drawn on eyebrows, the right one higher and more rounded than the left, giving her a permanent surprised look were missing too. A blank and wrinkled canvas stared back at me.

"You can't come in," she yelled. "I don't want you here."

My hands started to shake.

"I thought this would be over by now." Her wrinkles were now a shade of crimson.

"What would be over?" The gut feeling I had at the finding the door ajar had been right. Something was not as it should be.

"I just want to go to sleep. I'm so confused. I don't want to do this anymore," she cried.

For a split second a crack of lightening lit up the room. Booming thunder soon followed.

"That's why I came June, to help you get un-confused. We're going to get you some help." A landslide of boulders tumbled in my gut while an avalanche of unrecognizable thoughts roared through my brain.

"I don't want any help. I've had a good life. I don't want to do this anymore. I'm going to kill myself," she screamed as loud as her raspy, worn out vocal cords would allow.

Frozen. My feet stuck to the floor, arms stiff at my sides, but my brain raced a thousand hundred yard dashes, one right after the other, over and over. My own mother pulled this same stunt on her children many years ago, shortly after her divorce. I didn't know what to do about it then and I didn't know what I was supposed to do about it now.

The memory of Mom going off the deep end one spring day when both of my sisters were home from college and we were living in the apartment played out like a movie. Mom screamed and then threw the car keys at Susan saying she'd better take the car otherwise Mom was going to take it and drive it into a ditch so she could kill herself. Susan held me to shield me from the terror while she sobbed uncontrollably. Eventually the four of us left Mom at home and Susan with the keys in hand, ended up at the movie theater to see *Gone With the Wind*. It's a long movie and we even stayed to watch the credits. When we got back home, Mom was calm and cool and dinner was waiting for us on the table.

At a young age, I didn't understand the gravity my sisters felt, and that's why I used the word 'stunt' to describe it. My mother threatened many things as a way to keep us in line and I learned over the years I rarely had to take her seriously. Being the youngest, I exerted much more apathy over these threats than any of my siblings dared to do.

In this case however, the looming thunder and lightening added a menacing pall over the situation. I wondered if I had heard June correctly. I came to help her live out the rest of her life comfortably, not to find her dead in her bed. I've never seen a dead person except in a casket at a funeral. That's a far different experience than finding someone dead in his or her own home. I didn't really want June to be the first. Plus death at your own hand is pretty messy in my mind. Was June tricking me or was she serious? I wasn't able to tell.

Here I was standing in a dark hallway, in an apartment reeking of cigarette smoke, staring into a face that would scare the living daylights out of anyone in a Halloween haunted house, thinking what in the hell am I supposed to do now? I'm sorry dear Lord for swearing but I'm really at a loss right now. I came here to offer my assistance to get June organized and back in control of her life. Now I realized, I waited too long.

June pushed her way past me and sat down at the table in the kitchen. I followed. After lighting up a cigarette, she grabbed a note from the counter and forced it into my hand.

6/12/13

Dear Linda,

I'm sorry to leave things in such a mess. I'm totally confused and just want to go to sleep. I've had a good life. No regrets.

Have to smoke - no living facility. I've never smoked a cigarette I didn't enjoy.

No funeral and no obituary. Please respect my wishes.

I love you,

June

P.S. I'm well aware that smoking can shorten my life.

I'm sitting here while she blows smoke in my face reading her suicide note. That is not how I expected to be spending this time with June. I thought we'd stroll around Macy's together looking for some new clothes or go to her old haunt for dinner, Outback for a juicy steak. Instead I'm now in shock staring at a piece of paper reading what June wanted to be her final words to me.

Every Saturday at the grocery store, I waited for June to check out. She asked the cashier to get her a carton of cigarettes and usually suffered a lecture from the clerk or a person standing in line behind her.

She hated that. I did too. I never condoned tobacco and never took up the habit myself. That first illicit cigarette I tried as a teenager behind a bush down the street left me feeling sick to my stomach. No need for me to continue with a habit that left me wanting to throw up and not wanting any more. My mother took up smoking after her divorce. At the time, she said smoking made a divorcee look cool and sexy. Now I think about it, she tried desperately to keep up with June.

Sometimes I think people just need to shut up and mind their own business. Especially in the grocery store. What if she'd been overweight? Would they tell her not to buy the bag of potato chips, two blocks of cheddar cheese and a half-gallon of chocolate ice cream in her cart? I doubt it. They were just pissed because she held up the line by writing a check and asking the cashier to go to the service desk for the carton of poison while they not so patiently waited.

"I know you mean well, but I'm not leaving home." She pulled in a long drag on one of her signature skinny, slim cigarettes. "I'm sorry to do this to you." Smoked curled out from between her lips.

"How were you going to do it?" I asked, afraid she had a loaded gun tucked under her nightgown.

"I'll put a plastic bag over my head, pull it tight around my neck and that'll do it," she announced.

Obviously she gave this some thought. But a plastic bag? June loved to watch *Law and Order* and read mystery novels one right after the other. Tying a bag around her neck was the best she could come up with? Downing a bottle of Tylenol would have been a lot less painful and much easier. She had told me many times; she only wanted to go to sleep. That would do it.

"I want you to help me," she begged. She took another long drag, exhaling the smoke directly toward my face, no longer bothering to turn her head away from me in an act of polite smoking etiquette.

I stopped breathing, my heart ceased to beat. Frozen in place I stared seeing nothing. Not the swirling smoke rings, not the dirty dishes on the kitchen table, not the sad, droopy face calmly waiting for my answer. My body sat stiffly in the wobbly kitchen chair, my mind floated far away from the turmoil.

"June, I love you but I can't be a part of helping you kill yourself. I understand how hard this is and I only want you to be somewhere safe, where you don't have to worry about anything," I said. "Do you know what you are asking me to do?"

As much as I cared about June, I couldn't possibly help her end her life. She obviously wasn't thinking clearly if she thought I could. I understood she's angry and frustrated but after spending close to fifty years of our lives interacting with each other she knew me better than that.

She banged her fists on the table. "Then I want you to leave. Right now."

Just like that her mind took a u-turn from rational to erratic. Not that threatening suicide is rational, but she wasn't spitting nails at me when she explained her method of choice. Her eyes turned red and glared with anger. I stood, grabbed my suitcase and opened the door.

"Call me if you change your mind. Either way I'll be back in the morning."

With June's anger at such a fevered pitch, I feared she might strike out at me. In her fragile state, if I had to restrain her in any way she could go into a full blown cardiac arrest. I didn't want to end up in a physical fight and the way she pounded on the table I felt that was coming. She wanted to end her life right there and then in any way she could and morally I couldn't be a part of that. The child taught to respect the adult walked out afraid as a coward.

"I love you," a frail soft voice called out as the wheels of my suitcase clicked along the walkway. I didn't look back. I couldn't make myself do it.

"If you're going through hell, keep going."
— Winston Churchill

CHAPTER TWENTY-EIGHT

I found a hotel nearby with a room available for the night. Numb, I lay on the bed staring at the ceiling for what seemed like hours. Nothing in my life or in my relationship with June prepared me for this. My father, I thought, would be appalled. He'd say "Junie, you're being ridiculous," and she'd stop. Maybe she stewed for a while without showing it, but in the end it appeared to me, she did what he said. Even though I was my father's daughter, I never had that kind of power over my stepmother.

At some point, I got up, got ready for bed and crawled under the covers. My cell phone rang. I held my breath before answering it.

"Linda." It was June. "I'm not going to do it."

I heaved out a sigh of relief. "OK." I said.

"But I'm not leaving my house. Do you hear me?" She spit the words into the phone.

"I hear you June. I'll come over tomorrow and we'll talk about it," I said. I already had a schedule planned for the week and I wasn't cancelling anything that pertained to June and her care.

"I know you and Richard mean well but I don't need your help," she said.

"I love you, June. I'll see you tomorrow."

"I love you." Click went the phone.

This brief conversation was meant to give me some relief but it didn't. I relived the events of the day in my head. What could I have done differently? Should I have called the police since I feared she was a threat to herself? If I had stayed against her wishes, would she have hit me? I'd never seen her that angry. Would her anger have killed her in another way dispensing with the need of a plastic bag?

I recently read a column in the paper that the phrase "God only gives you as much as you can handle" is in reality grossly misquoted and misinterpreted from the actual Bible verse. The columnist believed this saying burdens people with a belief that God gave them their calamity. As he explained, the quote is a poor paraphrase of passage, which is more accurately paraphrased as: "God will not allow us to be tempted beyond our ability to escape." The verse is God's promise to provide us with an out in every temptation.

"Where dear God is my escape? Please show it to me soon so I can take care of June."

I found myself wondering whether I made a promise to my father the day before he died or if I simply took instruction on how to live my life. Either way, I struggled with understanding my moral code, the one that had been drilled into my head, that said I must obey my parents whether I agreed with them or not. Had June and I moved on from that long ago promise over the years in our relationship? Did we love each other as part of a family and as friends? Was I here to help her because I wanted to or because I felt an obligation? She needed me and I needed her. June had become the mother figure in my life and I had become her daughter.

I sucked in a deep breath. " Please dear God help June to find her escape from the misery she is in." I know she's miserable and she's lived a good long life and it takes too much energy to keep going on. Plus I don't think she knows where she is anymore. Nothing in her brain makes sense to her."

Sleep never came as I waited for a sign. I prayed over and over again that night that June was also patiently praying for her own path toward peace.

* * *

The next morning at 9 a.m, I knocked on June's door. She had a smile on her face, dressed, hair combed and eyebrows in place as she answered the door.

"Hey June. How are you?" I asked.

"I'm fine," she answered without a hint of the anger and despair she displayed yesterday. "Make yourself some coffee. I'll be out on the patio having a cigarette."

I made a cup of instant coffee in the microwave I bought her one Christmas that she insisted she didn't want or need and then proceeded to use every day. A small 600 watt countertop appliance became a miracle to an aging senior who suddenly found the stove and large oven a bit too much to manage, but didn't want to admit it. A microwave was a trip into the 21st century that it took her some time to make but made her glad when she finally did.

"I've got some errands to run this morning. Lanie from the Visiting Angels is coming at two," I said. June quietly sat with her legs crossed in a cheap plastic chair looking out at the view from her patio while puffing on a skinny cigarette. The tall pine trees gently swayed and even from the fifth floor, the movement of the pond could be seen.

"Who's Lanie?" she asked.

"She's from a service that provides home care for people like you who need a little extra help," I said.

"I can smoke?" she asked.

"Yes. She'll be here at two to ask you some questions," I answered. "I'm going to the grocery store. Do you want to come with me?"

"No." She sounded quite adamant about that, like I might whisk her away against her will if she left the confines of her apartment with me. "Take your key."

She's obsessed with me having the key. Now I'm afraid of a repeat of yesterday when she also made sure I had a key to let myself in while she was planning to be indisposed, as in dead. She wanted me to find her that way for some reason, and must have felt that I would be the only person to shed a tear for her, hold her hand for a time before sending her off without making a ruckus. She hated a lot of commotion. It's job I wouldn't relish but would accept for her at the right time and glad had not been bestowed upon me just yet.

I left her alone and went out as planned. The bank was the first stop where I gave them a copy of June's power of attorney so I could transact business for her. I initially only wanted to be added to her checking account so I could pay her bills but when I explained the situation to the customer service man at the credit union, he studied my documents for several minutes. His eyes intent on the page, I didn't want to interrupt him.

"She needs someone to take care of her. You should be added to all of her accounts," he said. "I'll go ahead and do that for you."

"OK," I answered meekly.

June had a few certificates of deposit and a checking account; that was it. I had no intention to take charge of it all because I didn't see it as necessary. One minute she was crazy and the next perfectly in control. I didn't do anything to stop my signature from being added. Later down the road, I thanked the bank employee over and over again for what he did even though at the time I thought he overstepped the rules.

Secondly I stopped at Wal-Mart for an elevated toilet seat and a couple grab bars for the shower. Next stop, the grocery store where I stocked up her refrigerator. We'd gone grocery shopping together for many years so I knew her food preferences pretty well. I threw in a half gallon of chocolate ice cream for good measure. She loved chocolate ice cream.

I brought home fried chicken, coleslaw and biscuits for lunch. It was far more than I wanted to eat, but June looked thin to me. I set the tiny kitchen table and called her in.

I put two pieces of chicken on her plate. Her false teeth sunk into the meaty leg tearing off a big chunk. She always liked the dark meat best. Richard had to fight her for the leg at Thanksgiving dinner every year since he loved it too. I always had more than enough white meat to satisfy me while I watched the two of them wrestle over the turkey legs.

"Tell your friend Lanie not to come," she flashed bits of chicken and her gold false teeth.

"I'm not going to cancel our appointment." Good try, June. Still reeling from the events of yesterday, I thought I better take all the plastic grocery bags I brought home from Publix straight to the trash room as soon as we finished eating lunch.

"This is still my house and I don't want her to come." She reached for the second piece of chicken, with her left hand while shoveling the coleslaw into her mouth with the right.

"June. You must have help, someone to wash your clothes and make you lunch. Wouldn't it be nice to have someone fix a meal so you didn't have to do it yourself?"

"I don't need help." The salad dressing dribbled down her chin.

"Your long term care insurance will help to pay for it," I said. "I can call the insurance company for you." June usually responded positively if I brought money into the equation.

I allowed these nonsensical arguments to frustrate me even though I knew in five minutes she wouldn't remember a single word. She proved that statement true over and over again yet I allowed our conversations to boggle me every time.

The phone rang at precisely two. Lanie called from the lobby.

"June. Lanie is here to talk to you. She's on her way up," I said.

"I can't wait to meet your friend," she answered cheerfully taking her place on the worn end of the sofa.

Lanie introduced herself to me at the door. I towered over her short stature. She was neatly dressed; professional yet casual with a crisp white blouse and navy blazer over cropped khaki pants and cute leather sandals.

"June. This is Lanie from the Visiting Angels. Remember I told you she was coming?"

"I remember," she said tersely to remind me she hadn't lost her marbles just yet. "It's nice to meet you."

Lanie asked if she could take a seat and June motioned for her to do so.

"Mrs. Wright, I'd like to ask you a few questions, if that's all right with you."

June nodded.

"What did you cook yourself for dinner last night?" she asked.

"I heated up some of the roast I had left over with potatoes and green beans. I have a microwave and it comes in very handy. Linda got it for me one Christmas. I use it all the time."

A roast? June loved to cook and try new recipes. She perfected an osso bucco dish she found in the paper many years ago. We had it so often at her table, Richard still talked about it. After my parent's divorce and the move to Seattle, June would cook all kinds of food for us when Steve and I spent our allotted three weeks of summer with them. Mom would be angry when we came back home, saying we had gained so much weight. I don't know if that was so much from June's cooking or the fact my father loved a good Dairy Queen cone and took us out for one almost every night.

Yesterday was the day we had all the commotion over plastic bags so I knew there was no leftover roast in the refrigerator but resolved myself to go along with the charade. I hoped Lanie had interviewed enough seniors tottering on the brink to know there wasn't a roast either.

The questioning continued about doctor's appointments, socializing, and when was the last time she'd done the laundry. June smiled and answered them confidently. She'd turned into a very proficient liar since I arrived.

"How do you get to the store to do your shopping?" Lanie asked.

"I have a driver. Ted. He takes me."

Ted lived in an apartment in the same building as June. She paid him to drive her to the store, the hairdresser and the doctor. She liked telling people she had "a driver". I guess it made her feel wealthy and sophisticated, neither of which she was or had ever been. She could be snooty, thinking she was better than everyone else. I learned that lesson over the years too.

"June, you're a remarkable woman," Lanie said to her. "How to you find your strength?"

"Trust in the Lord with all your heart and lean not on your own understanding. In all your ways acknowledge Him and He will make your paths straight." She rattled off the words of a bible verse from memory. They flowed off her tongue with ease.

I turned my head toward her. Never in all the time I knew her had I ever heard her mention God. It's not that I didn't believe she was a good and often kindhearted person capable of loving and caring for others. We never spoke about it. Dad only went to church when he had to, for a wedding or a funeral. Mom dragged all of us kids off to church every Sunday no matter what, whether we liked it or not. He refused to go and stayed home.

June had never shown the slightest interest in church or even a belief in God, at least not to me. I found her wallet later, after a time she finally relinquished her purse to me, stuffed with newspaper clippings and handwritten notes with prayers and sayings she saved over the years. Little tidbits that gave her strength were tucked away with a list of her prescription drugs, the phone number of the long-term care insurance company and a Publix check cashing card.

Little pieces of my heart began to crumble. All the love and energy we could have shared would now be lost. As an adult, I was also not a churchgoer but I found a spiritual energy deep within me that kept me going through good times and bad. If only we had found that bond between us earlier, maybe this part of our journey together could be easier, softer, and calmer.

"I never heard her say that before. June say that again. I like it."

Calmly June repeated the Proverb. Lanie reached for June's hand.

"Thank you for inviting me into your home. This was lovely," she said.

Lanie gathered up her things and I walked her to the front door.

"Let me see who I can find and I'll be in touch with you. Her smoking is problem, you know," she said. "She needs some shoes with some support. Has she been to a podiatrist recently?"

I explained I knew the shoes were not good but the family had been struggling to get her into a better fitting pair for years. "She's pretty stubborn, in case you haven't figured that out."

Lanie winked.

For the first time since I arrived, I felt relief, like I had made some progress.

* * *

I stayed with June a few more days to get things in order. I fed her and she ate like she'd been starving herself. She had been either forgetting to eat or subsisting on cheese and crackers since using the stove had become too difficult. She loved the elevated toilet seat, a fact I didn't need to know but she shared with me any way.

It's funny how now I began to realize the large number of secrets June managed to keep from me all the years we were having girlfriend chats over wine and dinner. I was under the impression we shared almost everything, talking and laughing like old friends. Now reality began to set in. June shared with me only what she thought I needed to hear. Our bond only a fragile thread stretched increasingly more thin through time.

Confident Lanie would send someone to be with June in a couple of days, I cancelled my appointment to visit a local assisted living facility in Boca Raton, and drove home. Exhausted and spent, I only wanted to crawl into my own bed and go to sleep. I fully intended to wake up the next morning ready to march on into whatever happened next, praying it would have nothing to do with death or smoking.

I started making lists of things to do. I called the doctor, the lawyer, and other assisted living homes near my home. I needed a back up plan too. I called Lanie to see how the search for June's companion was going. Her voice mail announced she'd be unavailable for the rest of the week. The receptionist at the Visiting Angels couldn't help. She couldn't find June's file. A strange and terrifying electrical jolt surge through my body.

Before I could think about what to do next, the phone rang.

Ted, the driver.

"I haven't driven her to the store in several weeks. She has to be out of food," he said.

"I was with her and stocked her up with food," I said.

"You were here?" he asked.

"I was with her for the past week," I answered.

Ted would not be the first person, nor would he be the last, to express surprise when I announced I'd been to see her. My first thought when this happened was if he was so concerned about her, why hadn't he shown up at her door or called while I was there? He lives in the same building so it's not that he has to go out of his way to knock on her door. Come to think of it, the entire visit, I ran into Rosemary only once. Joe and Darlene never called or came over either. None of the neighbors who she insisted were her friends made the slightest effort toward her.

Don't take this the wrong way. I get it that people are living far too busy lives to do my job for me, and I don't expect them to. But when they take the time to call me and tell me what I should be doing, I hope they have some first hand experience to relay to me. Am I expecting too much?

My next thought is he must think I'm a terrible person, and he, being the Good Samaritan has taken on the job of setting me straight.

"I don't think I can take her out anymore," he announced. "I'm 80 you know and I can't lift her anymore into my vehicle. I think she needs a wheelchair."

He's the one who drove her to the medical supply store to buy the walker that resides in the corner of the dining room gathering dust. Has he ever seen her use it to get around? Now he wants her to use a wheelchair. She wouldn't sit in it. In her mind a wheelchair labels her as old and disabled, neither of which she's willing to admit she is. Other people would see her as frail and feel pity. Her pride wouldn't let anyone think such a thing about her.

"Ted, you've been so kind to June over the years. I really appreciate all your help." I sucked in a deep breath before piling on more halfhearted compliments. "I completely understand if you don't want to drive her any longer. I'm trying to make some other arrangements for her. I'll start looking for another driver too."

"June's a nice lady. I enjoy talking with her when we go out," he said.

"Does she owe you any money? I'm paying all of her bills now," I asked.

"She does owe me forty dollars. She's out of cash, you know," he answered without a second of hesitation.

I took down Ted's address and phone and promised to send him a check. He says I can call him until I find someone else. I thanked him again for all he's done for her. I slam down the phone. He's just scammed me out of forty dollars and if he knows she's out of cash, he probably helped himself to that too. If mailing a check gets him off my back, it's a small price to pay to get him to go away.

As I walked down the path into elder care, I would come to know how important money was in the whole process of caring for the elderly. A whole segment of our economy now hinges on the care and service to elderly people who no longer posses the mental capacity to manage their own finances. They prey on the caretakers who are desperate to see their loved ones are well taken care of in their final phase of life.

Ted cashed his check promptly and I never heard from him again.

"Blame none, Linda, love all." –
The Universe

CHAPTER TWENTY-NINE

My cell phone rang about ten o'clock the next morning. June.

"Hello."

"Linda. I'm not moving. Don't make any more plans for me!" June said into the phone so loudly, I held it away from my ear. "I know you and Richard mean well but I'm not going."

Calmly I said, "I understand. I only want you to be safe."

"I have to have my cigarettes," she wailed and hung up the phone.

Less than ten minutes later, the phone rang again.

"Hi, June," I said.

"How did you know it was me?" she demanded.

"Your name popped up on the caller id," I answered knowing she had no idea what caller id was.

"I have to be able to smoke," her gravely voice roared into my ear.

"I understand. I only want you to be safe."

The phone went dead.

I waited another ten minutes and right on schedule the phone rang. I didn't even bother to say hello this time.

"Linda. What am I to do?" she cried, her breath hitched as she spoke.

"I want you to relax. I'm going to take care of everything for you," I said.

"Okay," she said. "Don't forget my cigarettes when you go to the store. I'm almost out."

"June, I'm at home. I can't bring you any cigarettes." I held my breath and waited for her response.

"Ooo." Her howling climbed to a high pitch. "How am I supposed to get cigarettes?"

"Call Joe and see if he'll go to the store for you."

Click went our connection.

June continued to call me every ten or fifteen minutes until about four in the afternoon. The calls stopped about the time she poured herself a vodka.

The calls persisted for the next three or four days, always beginning around ten a.m. and ending at the cocktail hour. I slept less and less each night thinking, praying, wondering what to do next. Lanie still hadn't returned my calls and I hadn't found a single assisted living home that would allow her to smoke.

"Loneliness is and always has been the central and inevitable experience of every man."
– Thomas Wolfe

CHAPTER THIRTY

When Lanie at the Visiting Angels never returned my calls, I had to take matters into my own hands and fast. I abandoned any plans to move June closer to me and found her a room at the Hawthorne Assisted Living down the street from June's apartment. Susan and Greg agreed to fly to Florida to do the extraction while I managed her move from afar.

June had been living at Hawthorne for about a month. She couldn't smoke there either but that ceased to be a high priority for me. The lobby was homey with a television and big comfy chairs. The rooms were clean and spacious, the staff friendly and helpful. It didn't come cheap but it was full of ladies like June who she could become friends with to divert her focus from me.

All my conversations with the nurses and Yvette, the concierge, indicated she was adjusting well. I tried to relax and grasp the idea I had done the right thing for her. That my father might be proud of me and know his Junie was being well taken care of came first.

I called her after dinner, like I did every few days.

"Linda. I'm so confused. I don't know what to do," she cried into my ear.

June frequently spoke of confusion but I'm not sure what she meant by that. I suspected people suffering from dementia, have a spot way down deep inside their brain, that clearly knows the mail is delivered every day at noon, the bills are paid by the act of writing a check, along with the names in order by age of all the children and grandchildren. The rest of their brain however, will not allow the person to verbalize those specific facts, creating a sense of confusion. That is how my non-scientific self explains how to decipher June's comments in a way that makes perfect sense to me, right or wrong.

"June, I'm taking care of everything for you. Just relax and enjoy yourself," I said.

"I don't have anyone to talk to. I'm so alone," she responded.

Running out of ideas on how to answer this question, I said nothing.

"I know you and Richard have good intentions, but this is horrible," she cried.

"June, give yourself some more time." I could hear her let out a long deep breath.

"Okay. I can do that." Her tone of voice calmed considerably. "When did you move away?"

"A long time ago, June." Her concept of time came and went like the hands on over wound clock with a spring loose.

"How long?" she wanted to know.

"Five years ago," I said.

"Oh, that's not very long to me," she replied.

I paused. Words that came out of June's mouth were beginning to confuse me about as much as they did her. Who really has the dementia? Is it the one whose brain is in turmoil? The words June speaks made perfect sense to her. Or is it the person trying to understand the mixed up thoughts of a person who is now in decline?

"What is a long time then?" I asked.

June answered quickly. "1966. The year I married your father." She let out a sad sigh. "I can remember it like it was yesterday. The best day of my life."

The thoughts of her Paul drove away all confusion in her world.

"Great is the human who has not lost his childlike heart." – Mencius

CHAPTER THIRTY-ONE

With tax season finally over, I spent more than enough time using the excuse I needed to recuperate from the exhaustion doing taxes could instill. As a CPA, tax preparation was the only job I could find but I really did enjoy it even though it only lasted for four months out of a year. It kept me busy and my mind off June.

The right thing for me to do now was to drive to Boca Raton and see Her. I hadn't been to see her since before Christmas when Richard and I drove to Ft. Lauderdale for a friend's boat parade party. I didn't want to do it but I'd run out of excuses.

What I was afraid of was that June would be thought of as a poor old woman with no family or friends. The nurses and staff at the home would feel sorry for her and when I did show up as infrequently as I did, they'd admonish me for the horrible, neglectful daughter that

I was. So here's where my struggle begins. Am I the daughter? Am I the cruel stepdaughter who only does exactly as much as she feels is required to get what's left of her money? The issue of blood relative versus a stepchild would not become apparent to me until much later. It played a huge role in her final care unbeknownst to me. Am I stupid or just plain naive?

When I felt I couldn't put a visit to June off any longer, it was Mother's Day. After driving the two and a half hours to see her, I stopped at Publix and picked up a pot of deep pink tulips and two bags of Dove Chocolates, her favorite, the kind with the little sayings inside the wrapper. They were on sale, buy one get one free. June always loved a buy one get one sale.

My nerves fluttered when I drove into the parking lot. Anything to do with June these days tended to put me on edge. Who inside would seek me out asking me to buy June some new clothes or tell me she was out of lipstick? I usually paid careful attention to a request from one of her aides, but the few times I showed up in person, they swarmed me like bees. I wondered if the shampoo and soap I sent ever got to June or if the nurse was out of it at home and had a black market going at the expense of the residents.

I found June stretched out on her bed staring at the ceiling. Her hair was done so I knew she at least got out of bed to go to the beauty parlor and her nails were painted a bright red. A manicure was something she'd never spent money on in her younger life. I paid the bill for it now and if it made her feel more pampered, I was glad to do it.

"Hi June. Happy Mother's Day," I greeted her with the tulips in my outstretched arms.

"I didn't know you were coming," she said. I called her three times in the past week to remind her.

"It's Mother's Day. I thought we should celebrate together," I replied.

"Isn't that nice of you." She sat up, took the plant, smelled the flowers and handed it back to me. "Tulips are my favorite."

"Mine too." I set them on her desk in the corner. "Can you see them from there?" I asked.

"Oh yes. That's perfect."

I set down the rest of my presents on June's chair, the one with the dark circular stain where, if I were guessing, pee would be if she couldn't get up in time and make it to the bathroom. She loved that chair and the little wood ottoman with the needlepoint cover that went with it. I had tried to clean it but couldn't get it out so maybe it wasn't pee at all, but something else I didn't want to think about. She insisted the chair come with her. So it did.

"Look what else I brought you." I waved the bag of chocolates in the air.

June smiled.

When I cleaned out her apartment, I found Dove chocolates of all different flavors tucked in a variety of places. I found them in with her underwear drawer, scattered among the orange foam curlers she rolled her hair in every night and even a couple in the medicine cabinet. Chocolate can cure just about anything so that's as good a place as any to keep some first aid.

"Scoot over." I climbed into the single bed she once hated but had now grown used to. Richard, being in the furniture business for most of his career, had picked her out a far better mattress than she ever slept on before. The new combinations of springs and memory foam cradled her aging bones. I relaxed.

"Milk chocolate or dark with caramel?"

June held out her hand. "Whatever you're having."

I opened the dark chocolate, handed one to June and took one for myself. June unwrapped the sweet and greedily ate it before reaching for another.

"Wait, what did your fortune say inside the wrapper," I asked.

The small black printing on the foil proved difficult for her aging eyes to read. She held it close, straightened her arm to move it farther away, before turning it to the right.

"I can't read it. What does it say?" she asked in a phelgmy voice coated in chocolate. "Where's my water?"

A small, short bottle of water lived on her nightstand. I handed it to her and she took a long gulp.

"Be good to yourself today," I read from the wrapper.

"OK, I can do that. What's yours say?" she asked.

"Go ahead. Have another." We both giggled.

I reached into the bag and gave us each two more candies.

We stretched out on the bed, talking and laughing like two young girls at a sleepover. I'm never sure which June I'd get when I called or visited. I've felt the wrath of cranky, dementia ridden June and happy June is much more fun to be with. Today was a good day, calm, peaceful and most of all happy.

By the time I took a good look in the bag, only a handful of chocolates remained. While we were solving the problems of the world for well over an hour, we'd managed to polish off a bag of candy.

"I'll put what's left in your drawer. You can have some before you go to bed," I said. "I better because you'll go to dinner soon. So let's have one for the road."

June unwrapped it and read from the wrapper herself this time.

"Enjoy this moment," she whispered.

I bent down to hug her thin frail shoulders and kissed her on the cheek. She hugged me back.

"I'll see you tomorrow, Ok?" Her eyes glistened, filled with tears.

"Ok. I love you," she said.

"I love you too," I answered back.

"Before Alice got to Wonderland, she had to fall."

CHAPTER THIRTY-TWO

The next month my routine interaction with June changed dramatically. I went back to work full time. My days were no longer my own as I tried to learn the ropes at a small securities office. My medical insurance became too pricey and I struggled to pay the premiums while attempting to keep my retirement funds intact. I needed employer-sponsored benefits and full time work was the only way to get them.

Richard called me the girl who can't wait to get old. His social security check came right on time every month with his Medicare premium already deducted. I longed to be able to retire along side him but with thirteen years difference in our ages, I had some catching up to do.

Even though June lived 150 miles away, I'd never been in the habit of visiting her on the weekends. I dreaded the drive and I learned to check on things by phone. I talked to Yvette, the concierge, who answered the phone at Hawthorne several times a week. I thought I was getting accurate information about June's condition and was in touch enough for the staff to be aware someone watched over her.

"Mom's okay," said the voice on the other end of the phone. Those two words were to become the new salutation I would hear over and over again any time I received a call about her regardless of the situation. "She fell in the bathroom this morning. Her aide found her and she went by ambulance to West Boca Medical Center."

"Do you know how she is?" I asked.

"I don't know anything," the nurse at Hawthorne replied. "The hospital has been given your contact information."

"Thank you. I'll call the hospital."

A call to the hospital meant a maddening trip through an electronic maze called a switchboard. Press one for this, press two for that. I listened to each number until I got to "press nine for an operator". The operator transferred me to the surgical floor. I was put on hold three more times before I finally spoke to a nurse who knew of June. She hadn't yet been assigned to a room but she would be admitted sometime today.

"Fracture of the left hip," she said before transferring me back to emergency.

The frustration at getting through on a phone was about to pale compared to what was coming next.

"Do you have a power of attorney?" the emergency room nurse asked.

"Yes."

"Fax it to me. I can't discuss anything with you until I have it on file," she announced.

I wrote down the fax number and got the wrinkled, faded document out of my file folder. June made me her power of attorney after my father died. The signed paper was tucked away in my file cabinet for years just waiting for the opportunity to show its face. The bank and the assisted living home made use of it. This necessary and previously unused legal agreement was about to make the rounds in a big way.

The orthopedic surgeon called a couple hours later after I stewed myself into an overcooked soup.

"Mrs. Wright has a fracture of the left hip. You have two choices," he said. "We can do a hip replacement or we can keep her off it until it heals on its own."

"What are the pros and cons of each? She's 92 years old," I asked.

"Only a third of women over age 80, survive more than a year after a hip replacement. Not having the replacement means she's bed ridden and runs the risk of bed sores." He continued on with a lot of technical jargon intended to help me make a decision. My brain turned to mush and I tuned it all out. Here I was in charge of making the life or death choice for another person for the second time in my life.

"Are you her daughter?" he asked. "Are you able to sign consent forms for Mrs. Wright?

"Stepdaughter," I answered and waited. "I can sign. I have her power of attorney."

"Do you need some time to think it over?" the doctor asked.

All she wants is for all this to stop, to be with Paul, my Dad, her husband. No matter what choice I make, the good qualities of life ended for her long ago. I was making a decision on how miserable her final days were going to be. Would one choice bring death sooner than the other? I had no way of knowing.

I chose a hip replacement. I prayed I wouldn't regret it later. My siblings made it clear from the start, decisions about June were mine to make.

* * *

June's surgery took place the next afternoon. The doctor called me around 4 o'clock.

"Everything went well," he said. "Her bones are thin so I had to wire the bones to the prosthetic. Nothing to be alarmed about. It's fairly common."

I wouldn't fully understand until I had my own hip replacement a few months later at age 60. My surgeon gave me some background on this, I think as part of the usual protocol of keeping the patient informed. It's unknown how a person's bones will react to the new hip until it's put in. The bone may spread and in that case the wire is used to hold things together.

"She's going to spend the night in ICU mainly because of her age," he added. "The floor nurse will call you when she moves to a regular room."

I thanked the doctor and put down the phone. I held my face in my hands wondering what I needed to do. Just like June I thought, "What am I to do?" only I had no one to calm or reassure me by saying, "Relax and enjoy yourself".

The next day the floor nurse called right on schedule and asked for the power of attorney. I dutifully faxed it to her for June's file.

Not having been in a hospital since 1980, I didn't realize how much things had changed. Each patient is assigned a nurse and the patient's relatives call that nurse's cell phone if they need anything. I knew June couldn't reach the phone next to her bed so I called the nurse instead.

"I want to make sure she has her teeth and her wedding ring," I said to the nurse on duty that evening. "They were supposed to be kept on the floor until she got moved back."

Does a hospital have a locker for such things as dentures, glass eyes, toupees that had to be removed before going into the operating room. Did patients forget to ask for them back? Did they die and not need these items any longer? Did their grieving families not know of the existence of such personal items and therefore not retrieve them? Then what happened? Did the hospital hold a once a year lost and found rummage sale?

Teeth for sale. Well used.

See clearly again. Glasses in every prescription. One is sure to be perfect for you or someone in your family.

I never saw June's false teeth except when they were in her mouth, and I didn't want to see them any other way. But having her gum her food for the rest of her life was equally as disturbing to me.

"Let me check for you. Mrs. Wright, smile for me." There was a pause. "She's got her teeth."

"What about her ring? It's just a plain gold band." I said.

"Mrs. Wright. Do you have your wedding ring? Hold up your hands."

I could hear June start to wail in the background. "My ring! My precious ring. Where is it?" She sobbed loudly. "My precious ring."

"She only has one ring. No diamonds." I said.

Hawthorne had banned all her good jewelry when she moved there. It had been sent to Robin, the niece who never even had the good manners to say thank you, or even to say that the package had arrived at her doorstep.

"Waaa. Woo, where is my ring?" June screamed now. "My precious wedding ring."

"I'm sorry to do this to you," I offered as consolation to the nurse. Why couldn't she nonchalantly hold her hand and look for the ring with out speaking. Even I knew she was asking for trouble when she said, "Hold up your hands."

"She's wearing the gold band."

The howling continued.

"Thank you. I appreciate all the hard work you do to care for her."

I hung up the phone figuring it might be time for her shot of pain medication and the nurse would now want to get to into her as soon as possible to stop the ear piercing wailing that would keep the entire floor of patients awake all night.

That weekend, Richard and I drove to Boca to see her. In the mean time I spoke with the social worker at the hospital who gave me a list of nursing homes with beds available for her. Hawthorne was an assisted living home that required her to be ambulatory in order to stay. June now needed a skilled nursing home with round the clock care.

I scoured the Internet for reviews, which were not much help. Some people loved a facility saying their parent had received wonderful care, and just as many took the other view with a one star rating and a tale of gross proportions. I finally called the director at Hawthorne for some advice. She offered that Dr. Mandel, the doctor at Hawthorne who cared for June was on staff at the Forum. At least she might recognize a familiar face or voice.

June looked like a withered tree branch in the middle of her hospital bed; small and weathered, when we arrived at her bedside. Asleep, I reached for her hand. Her eyes opened and she smiled.

"Linda."

"Hi, June. How are you?" I asked.

"I'm getting really good care here, aren't I?" she asked.

"I think so," I said with a smile.

An aide arrived with her lunch tray. I raised up the head of the bed for her and helped to get her comfortable. I spread the napkin on her lap, unwrapped the flatware and removed the cover from the steaming hot chicken soup.

Suddenly my stomach growled and if I was hungry, that meant Richard must be starving. He had a perpetual hollow leg that needed to be filled on a regular schedule. June slurped down her soup and moved on to the chicken salad and pita bread.

"Who's that man over there?" she asked with bits of chicken falling over her lips.

"That's Richard," I answered.

"Have I met him before?" she asked.

"He's my husband. You came to our wedding." Maybe a memory jolt would get her back into line mentally. Richard chuckled in the background.

"Oh. Okay." June discovered the cup of chocolate ice cream on her tray and ripped the top of all by herself. Chocolate ice cream was her favorite. She never bought a box of cereal for herself since that would require milk. She never drank milk or ate yogurt and steered away from dairy products in general. Set a dish of chocolate ice cream in front of her and in a minute flat she licked the bowl clean. Expensive store bought or from the hospital freezer, it made no difference to her.

"Mrs. Wright, you were hungry!" The nurse scanned the empty plates on the tray before pushing it to the side. "I'm going to freshen up your sheets, so I'm going to roll you on your side. Is that okay."

"Can you just put a bag over my head and put me out of my misery?" June asked.

"What! Do you want me to go to jail?" the woman exclaimed.

This was another laugh or cry moment for me. June only wanted help and didn't care if someone else would go to prison. If she got assistance from anyone, she'd be dead right now instead of lying in a hospital bed wearing a skimpy gown. She'd get what she wanted and it wouldn't matter one bit what happened to her accomplice.

I still remember vividly the day she threatened suicide. It's a secret I've kept from the rest of the family all this time. It's painful. I still can't make sense of the sane mind or the demented mind and which is controlling what.

Obviously it's on June's mind. She hasn't moved on from the bag either. I always thought she was a smart enough woman to figure out a handful of pills would complete the task much more efficiently. Somewhere in her mind she's not able to comprehend that honest people can't help her kill herself. Prison is not a place on our bucket list.

Richard stood in the corner giggling at the scene in front of him. He knew the story of June and her plastic bag and had kept that secret at my request. To see her lying in the hospital bed trying to find other accomplices meant she watched too many crime shows on television. Those were the shows she loved to watch the most and their impact seems to be at the forefront of her thinking process. Funny how our brains work.

In a clean bed, June promptly fell asleep. I sat by her bedside, held her hand and gently rubbed it with my thumb back and forth. A peaceful face smiled back at me.

I stopped at the nurse's station to see if they needed anything from me and to tell them we'd be back tomorrow. One of them waved and immediately put her nose back to the task she'd been in the middle of at a computer.

Armed with my list of nursing homes, the hospital social worker had suggested, we got back in the car. First we stopped at Burger King for a Whopper before finding our way to the Forum at Deer Creek where Dr. Mandel would be the one and only familiar face. Since June spent more than three days in the hospital, Medicare would cover the first 20 days of skilled nursing care. I'd managed not to dig too deeply into her savings during her year and half at Hawthorne, but this would be a whole new ballgame as far as finances were concerned.

I introduced myself at the front desk explaining why I was there and asked for a tour.

"Absolutely. Let me call someone to show you around," the receptionist said.

Richard and I wandered uncomfortably around the reception area. A bulletin board posted upcoming events, a potluck on Tuesday, a bus trip to the mall and a note to say good-bye to a long time worker in the kitchen.

The sound of a woman's voice reading caught my attention. She sat at the head of a long table with about ten elderly residents seated around it. A book was open and she read out loud with inflection and passion. No one listened. The women mainly hung their heads forward, chin resting on chest. The men tilted their heads back; mouths wide open, exerting a small snort every now and then.

"Is this what we should look forward to?" Richard snuck up behind me and assessed the scene in front of us.

"Don't worry. I'm going to start stockpiling the pills as soon as we get home," I told him.

We both laughed. We were getting a lesson in how to plan for our own end of life care as difficult as it appeared.

If I learned anything so far walking down this path with June, it was that I didn't want to be in her shoes when I got to be her age. I wanted to take care of myself before I got to the point of no return and unable to think clearly. Everything would be in place. Like June, I have a stepdaughter but since she lives a thousand miles away, I've no hopes of her coming to my rescue in my old age. Unlike June and me, and due to the difference in age of Richard and me, Pam is only eleven years younger. We'll be headed to the old folks home about the same time. June assumed someone would watch out for her, and no one did. For myself, I wanted to make sure I didn't hang a ten-ton guilt trip on anyone else, like June had on me.

We're all on a train and everyone knows the last stop is Death Valley. The conductor collected our ticket on the day we were born. There are no other stops between here and the end of the line, so we can't pull the cord alerting the driver to stop. We're stuck. It's beginning to become hot and dusty, the grit and grime fills our eyes, leaving us unable to see the beauty of the life we once knew. Death Valley's a welcome stop any way we look at it, but I'm anxious for us to arrive, as is June. So we sit and wait. We can't speed up the train and there's no arrival time on the timetable to look forward to.

A family member told me once I had no obligation to take care June. Don't I have a moral responsibility to take care of someone who's been a part of my life for fifty years? As a society, shouldn't we make a commitment to protect others, young or old when they're unable to care for themselves regardless of who they are or whether their blood runs through our veins? The distinction we make between ourselves and other people is made in our minds, choosing what we want to believe. In the end we all want the same thing out of life, food, clothing, shelter and safety. With safety comes love.

Are the families of the men and women sleeping through the book club, agonizing any less than I am because they had to put their parents in a nursing home? I doubt it. They are passengers on the slow train too. No one comes to this decision lightly. I could only hope wherever I did send her, she would be cared for in a way I was unable to do.

A cheerful young woman appeared to give us our tour, allowing me escape from my dreary thoughts if even for only a few minutes.

"Here's our physical therapy room."

Richard and I looked around at the weights and balls, treadmills and stationery bicycles and nodded to each other with approval. We did the same at the dining room, television lounge, and card room.

"Here is one of our patient rooms." She raised her arm indicating we could go in.

The room was spacious, with a large window allowing in the sunlight. The beds were neatly made with blue and green matching bedspreads. Each had a nightstand and an overhead lamp. I wouldn't want to live here but it seemed pleasant enough for a nursing home.

With our tour over, we thanked our guide and left.

"What do you think?" I asked Richard. "It didn't smell like pee."

"I can't smell remember?" he answered. "It's fine."

The decision was made. June would come here to recuperate from her hip replacement.

"Forget the mistake. Remember the lesson."

CHAPTER THIRTY-THREE

"Does she need clothes?" I asked the too young sounding to have such a job, hospital social worker while making the arrangements to move June to the nursing home.

"No, she doesn't need any clothes," she answered.

Through all this I always worried whether she had clothes to wear. She certainly wasn't any kind of fashion plate in these later years with her pull on pants ordered from an old ladies catalog and pull over t-shirts in every color of the rainbow. All the items on sale in the mail order catalog she loved were plain and button-less. Not a button appeared on any page, only an occasional snap but lots of elastic, on waistbands and cuffs. Pullovers and pull ons were all the rage according to the full color advertisements I now found in my mailbox after having her mail forwarded to my home address.

One of the selling points of the Hawthorne Assisted Living was once weekly laundry service. I paid attention to that because June, who had spent her career buying dresses for a variety of department stores, had stopped worrying about how she looked. Her morning coffee usually found its way down the front of her shirt. I had no way of knowing if it was this morning's coffee or last week's. She wore the same shirt over and over again.

When I visited and looked in the closet, I saw all kinds of fancy, colorful print tops and I had no idea where they'd come from.

June brushed off my questions. "Every time they take my laundry, different clothes come back. They're not mine."

"Do you wear them?"

June turned her head toward the blaring television and pretended not to hear me.

The pants hanging in the closet, however, were the same stretch waist, polyester in boring colors of black, gray and navy. How the staff could keep the pants straight but not the tops mystified me. Maybe they washed the pants separately because of all the pee and poop the Depends didn't catch. I'm sure there had to be something clinging to the fabric.

After I hung up my call with the teenager masquerading as an adult with a college degree in social work, I called Yvette. I didn't understand why she wouldn't need anything to wear. June would not be happy lying around in a hospital gown all day.

"Yvette, how can I get some clothes for June over to the Forum? June's going there for rehab," I asked in a calm, sweet voice.

"I think Cindy, one of our volunteers, lives near there. I'll see what I can arrange for you," she said.

As soon as I hung up the phone, I put two Visa gift cards in the mail to say thank you. Money talks, I learned, when it came to elder care. Since I couldn't be close to do these chores for her, I had no choice but to rely on the power of money. These workers I had come to know over time, were happy to help because they knew the generous check was in the mail.

* * *

June had been in rehab for about two weeks when I got a call late at night from the on-duty nurse.

"Mom's okay. She's going back to the hospital. Her incision is infected and antibiotics are not clearing it up," she said.

"Is she going back to West Boca Medical Center?" I asked. In the back of my mind, I hoped I wouldn't have to fax the power of attorney again.

"Yes. They will start her on intravenous antibiotics. The doctor will call you in the morning."

I thanked her and tried to get back to sleep. Tomorrow would turn out to be a very long day.

The orthopedic doctor was the first to call.

"She has an infection. I need to operate and clean it up." He went into all the medical reasons for the additional surgery and they flew right over my head. "This is not uncommon in people her age."

Did I pick incorrectly? Maybe a bedsore might be less traumatic for her than two surgeries in the span of two weeks and a festering infection.

I agreed to the surgery. Within minutes a nurse called.

"Can you fax me your power of attorney?"

I literally carried the document wherever I went these days. She had her fax in a matter of minutes and I was safe to make appropriate decisions for June once again. Proper choices or not, I was once again in charge.

The surgery went well and that night I did the teeth and ring check again with a different nurse who knew enough to look for these items rather than ask a loud, demented old woman to show them to her.

Five o'clock the next morning a ringing phone woke me out of the sound sleep I had only been in for an hour. From two until after four, I stared at the clock wondering when sleep would come. Counting sheep was no help these days.

"Mom's okay. She needs a blood transfusion."

I began to understand that health care workers were trained to start every call concerning elderly patients with the phrase "Mom's okay" or "Dad's okay" to dispel panic during early morning or late night calls.

"Why?" I asked in my half awake stupor.

"Her blood count is very low due to the infection. Dr Mandel ordered it," the nurse said.

"Is it necessary? I don't want any heroic measures." I said.

"It's necessary according to the doctor," she responded.

"Can you ask the doctor to call me? I want to talk to him first before I give the authorization." I suddenly felt important and in charge by not agreeing right off the bat with the forceful and demanding health care professional.

She took down my cell number and my head fell back on the pillow. I stared at the ceiling wondering if this would be the day, all of this could end for June. I'm certain that's what she would want. How many hospital workers would she ask to put a bag over her head before that would happen naturally? Mother Nature had been given plenty of clues but so far had refused to give June what she wanted. That remained in my control, exactly where I didn't want it to be.

Driving to work, the phone rang. My car has Bluetooth so I was able to answer and talk through the car speakers. Even though Florida doesn't have a cell phone law, hands free talking is a technological miracle for a baby boomer like me.

"Linda, Dr. Mandel here. How are you?" He spoke with an accent so I knew English wasn't his first language. He was pleasant no matter what the conversation was about.

"I'm fine. More importantly, how's June?" I asked.

"She needs a blood transfusion. Her blood count is very low," he answered.

"I don't want any heroic measure for her. She's suffered enough."

Dr. Mandel's voice took on a different tone, like I was being ridiculous even saying such a thing.

"There is nothing heroic about a blood transfusion. Her blood count is very low. It will help her fight the infection," he said.

I backed down and agreed to the treatment. I felt worn down and frankly; I was tired of playing God. It's God's turn to play God.

Then the doctor said, "Did you know she has a mass on her lungs? Do you want to treat it?"

"How did you find that?" I asked.

"We did an MRI. Was she a smoker?" he responded.

When she moved into the assisted living apartment and her cigarettes were no longer accessible to her, I begged the nurse to get her something for the withdrawal. Here I am speaking to the same doctor who has been caring for her all this time, almost two years and nothing in her chart says she smoked. Anger began to boil up inside me but I couldn't decide who to direct it to, the forgetful or unsympathetic nurse, our fractured healthcare system or an unprepared doctor who doesn't have all the information he needs to properly treat his patients.

"Doctor, she smoked since she was fifteen years old. She never had a cigarette she didn't enjoy," I answered trying to keep the edge off my voice. "No, I don't want to treat it. She's ninety three." Her age alone was enough justification to make that decision.

"I understand. Please call me if you have any other questions," he politely answered before disconnecting the call.

The workday plodded along with the conversation with the doctor running over and over in my head. I still hadn't come to terms with whether or not I had made the right decisions. Everyone must look at me like a murderer. The Hippocratic Oath that every doctor has taken says they will treat the patient to the best of their ability and judgment. Nowhere in the oath does it say anything about helping an old, sick patient to die. They don't want to make those decisions either, so they are leaving them to my emotional and confused heart.

Driving home after work my phone rang again.

"Is this Linda Wright?" a voice asked.

"Yes." I answered.

My name is Sandy. I'm June Wright's nurse at West Boca Medical Center," she paused. "June would like to speak to you."

The next sound I heard rattled me so hard I barely missed driving off the road.

"Liiiinddddaaa! Where are you?" June yelled.

"June. I'm at work." I lied.

"Okay," she replied in a normal tone of voice.

"How are you feeling today?" I asked.

"I've been better. Why don't you come to see me?" The sharp edge of her words started to return.

"June, I go to work every day." I learned during our journey through dementia and old age that on some level she still understood it was necessary for me to work. She didn't ever argue with me when I mentioned work. She'd been an independent woman even after she married Dad.

"I need you. I need you to talk to," she whined.

"You have to concentrate on getting better. I'll come down and see you next weekend," I said.

My father taught me the Golden Rule, Do Unto Others as You Would Have Others Do Unto You. All these lies I had to tell went against everything I'd been raised to be. A jolt ran up my spine each time I spoke an untruth to pacify June. This time tears ran freely down my face.

The nurse got back on the phone. June wailed unintelligible thoughts in the background.

"I know how hard this is," she offered some compassion to me.

"I wish I knew what to do for her. Thank you for taking care of her," I said.

"She's a sweet lady. She'll be fine. Don't worry."

Unable to stop the tears of frustration before I pulled into the garage, Richard stared at me when I came through the door.

"I just got off the phone with June" I said.

"What did she want?" Richard asked as he flipped a piece of fish in the fry pan cooking on the stove.

"She screamed at me and wanted to know where I was," I said, tears beginning to run down my cheeks again. "You know how she says 'Linda' when she's really angry at me."

Richard had known her for over twenty-five years and broke out into a fit of laughter when I imitated the screech of her voice. I couldn't help but join him in laughing at how ridiculous our conversation became when repeated in a made up version of June's hoarse voice. I found myself in another one of those laugh or cry moments. If I didn't laugh, I'd cry until I ran out of tears.

"We can't help everyone, but everyone can help someone."

CHAPTER THIRTY-FOUR

I periodically sent an information update on June to Susan since she was the only one of my sisters involved in any way in what was happening with our stepmother. The few days after receiving one of my frustrating messages, Susan called me. I was still getting used to that. We weren't the sisters to call each other up just to talk, ever. Suddenly I had both her cell phone and her unlisted home phone saved in speed dial. It took some getting used to her schedule. If I called before nine in the morning, Greg answered since Susan was still sleeping. My day started at six thirty a.m., rain or shine, seven days a week. I couldn't make sense of a seventy-year-old woman still having teenage sleeping habits.

She and Greg had been to visit June. They own a winter home in Naples and made the two hour trip across Alligator Alley to see her for a couple hours. Sometimes if I knew they were making a visit, I asked them to take her something she needed. This time June had been in the nursing home for close to two months and wasn't making any forward progress with her hip.

"June said to tell Linda not to sign her up for any more classes. She doesn't want to go," Susan said.

"Classes? What classes?" I asked. What came to mind was the room full of sleeping seniors at book club, Richard and I witnessed on our scouting trip to the nursing home.

"I think it's the physical therapy. She was coming back to her room when we got there." Susan said.

"Is she walking?" I asked

"No. Obviously, she's not paying attention in class," Susan joked.

"Obviously she's not," I laughed too.

The next day I called and asked to speak with the physical therapist. Lisa greeted me cheerfully.

"How is June Wright doing with her physical therapy?" I asked.

"June is still not able to stand for more than a few seconds," she said. "We've been working with her but she's very weak."

"Do you think she will be able to stand or walk again?" I asked.

Lisa hesitated for a minute and then carefully chose her words.

"I'm not confident therapy is helping her any longer," she said.

Right then I heard June's message. Cancel class. She would happily take the F on her report card.

My next call was to Sherry, the nursing home administrator.

"Sherry, I want June placed in hospice care." I'd been thinking about doing this for some time. June didn't have the strength or the energy to keep fighting and hadn't for a long time. She knew I was the one in charge of her life. June hadn't forgotten me and the job she had given me, or the job my father had given me on her behalf.

"She still has thirty two more days of care paid for by Medicare," Sherry responded. "We ordered her a knee brace to see if that would help with her leg strength. Her left knee is twisted in, you know."

Sherry's job was to keep the bed occupied and the bill paid. As long as she could keep Medicare paying, she was going to do it. The two of us had butted heads before over June. Sherry had a commanding attitude and I believe she thought she could get away with something like this since I wasn't nearby and hadn't done any pop in visits lately.

"Sherry, why didn't you consult me before you spent the government's money on a brace for her? Her knee has been like that for close to forty years. That's not what's preventing her from standing."

"A brace is the protocol once the standard care options have been exhausted." She had an answer for everything.

"I want her put on hospice care as soon as possible," I demanded. I knew hospice would not bring an immediate end to June's life, but it would stop unnecessary therapy and exhausting visits to doctor's offices. It may give her some emotional support to move more gently toward the end of her life.

"That means she'll go on self pay. Medicare is still paying so she needs to continue the therapy until that time is exhausted."

"I spoke to Lisa and the therapy isn't helping. I want her on hospice as soon as possible. What do I need to do to make that happen?" I was losing my patience.

"I want to see June's financial statement. We do not accept Medicaid at this facility," she replied.

Here we go again. It's all about the money. I should know that by now.

I faxed June's most recent bank statement showing she had approximately two hundred thousand dollars left since the sale of her condominium and a long term care policy that paid $120 a day toward her care. June was one of the lucky ones. She had a financial cushion to keep her comfortable, at least for a while.

Sherry approved June to stay within minutes.

I read a statistic 59% of assisted living residents eventually move to a skilled nursing facility. I can add June to that list. The average stay in a nursing home is 835 days or 27.8 months. Sherry is charging me $8,000 a month for June's bed times 27.8 months means according to the statistics June has enough money to last.

Popping into my head, I saw June's red and scrunched up face. She begged me not to move her to a facility. I wish I could find another word for 'facility' because June called every place that interred old people a facility. The word painted a picture of a long sterile corridor where the walls are covered in gleaming stainless steel. A person is wheeled in one end before the doors lock tight behind them and are pushed out the other end in a body bag. What happens in between is anyone's guess. I've not been able to find a suitable substitute for the word facility. That's where she was and where she was going to stay. June knew more than I gave her credit for.

"Will my family forgive me for not leaving them any money?" she cried to me shortly after she moved into assisted living.

"You saved your money to take care of yourself. They'll forgive you." I did my best to pacify her.

My father had a saying as he spent his last nickel; they'd be nailing his coffin shut. His children had no expectation of money falling into their pockets because he had died. And it didn't. I wasn't part of the family June worried about. The mysterious niece and nephews lurked in the background never appearing in the flesh, only lying in wait to see how big the check would be.

*"It's not the cough that carries you off.
It's the coffin they carry you off in."
— Old family saying*

CHAPTER THIRTY-FIVE

"Pastor Gordon called today," Richard announced when I got home one afternoon.

"Who's he?" I asked.

"He's from hospice. He went to see June today."

"That's nice," I said.

"He wants to speak to you. Does June have a prepaid funeral plan?" Richard asked.

"I don't think so. I'll go look in her book," I said.

I referred to June's trusty book I bought her years ago, many times. I didn't always find what I was looking for but sometimes I got lucky. The page I located near the back of the book was titled 'The Final Dress Rehearsal'. I don't know why anyone would call a funeral a dress rehearsal. It's the real thing, final, because the person who is the center of attention at a funeral is dead and gone. It's the last party thrown in their honor.

A person doesn't get to lie down in their coffin, hold their breath and then listen to make sure their chosen death march is played in tune. When it's over and the person sits up, scares the crap out of the mourners, they don't get to walk into the funeral directors office and tweak what they didn't like about the service so it can be improved for the real deal.

I knew June didn't want any kind of service but someone had to come haul her body away when the bittersweet goodnight arrived. She had written, "Advance arrangements have been made with Kraeer Funeral Home." in the book. The address was listed along with a phone number. The next line was curious to me. " Copy of vital statistics on file with them and also in steel box". A document labeled as 'vital statistics' is either a birth certificate or a death certificate and June's not dead yet. Why a funeral home would require a birth certificate left me wondering.

The second part of my search started in her steel box, the one I had also brought home with me after I cleaned out her apartment. It contained another treasure trove of personal papers and notes that were able to instantly invoke sharp emotions. I'd been through this box many times, most of the papers old and no longer valid. This time I searched for her vital statistics, whatever that might be.

The only thing I found with that specific title was my father's death certificate. Kraeer Funeral home in Boca Raton handled his cremation and funeral. While June allowed me to make the life and death decision for my father, she took complete control of the funeral preparation.

I drove her to the funeral home the day after we returned from Miami. I remember sitting in front of a tiny wood desk littered with papers talking to a very large man in a red jacket who was the funeral director. He loomed over us like the professional wrestler, Andre the Giant.

June picked out the flowers, the minister and the room to rent, including the number of chairs she expected to fill for the service. The funeral director explained the burial at sea she requested for his ashes. Andre the Giant had convinced her Sunday was the best day for a funeral, people had nothing else to do on a Sunday afternoon, and she could expect a bigger turnout. The minister was available. His Lutheran congregation retired him a few years back. Andre entered the items they agreed upon on a form, adding up the prices and totaling the charges.

"Mrs. Wright, the cost will be three thousand, two hundred and fifty dollars," he said.

June turned and looked at me. "I don't have that much money. How am I going to pay for it?"

"We'll put it on your credit card and figure it out later," I said. That's how I handled my finances. I kept emergency funds out of everyday reach and would transfer the money when to bill came. I assumed my father would have done the same thing.

Andre the Giant gasped. "I don't want you to use your credit card. We'll figure out a payment plan for you."

He didn't want to take a credit card knowing he would add another three percent onto the balance to cover the credit card fee. A payment plan would be far more lucrative for him by collecting interest from June each and every month for two or three years. I was cynical about people's money motives even back then and June was only sixty-nine years old at the time.

"Oh wait," she yelled out. "Your father gave me a check for my Christmas present. I can use that."

"What?" I asked.

"Mrs. Wright, I don't want you to spend a Christmas present on a funeral," Andre tilted his chin downward in an effort to show his compassionate side.

I sure as hell hoped she had already cashed this check but I doubted it with all that had happened in the past week. For once, through all this I was glad it was the holidays. Hopefully the bank wouldn't find out Dad was dead and freeze his accounts before June could negotiate the Christmas gift turned into funeral payment. We'd stop at the bank on the way home.

June and Andre the Giant made arrangements to bring the check on Sunday before the service. He was kind enough to get everything ready and delay her payment since it was Christmas. He couldn't have lain on any thicker how generous he was being by giving her this reprieve and June fell for it hook line and sinker.

Not finding anything from the funeral home for her own funeral, I called the number in her book. Twenty-five years later, Kraeer Funeral Homes had been sold to a big company that had snapped up little mom and pop undertakers who were drowning in today's economy.

The large welcoming two-story white clapboard house with green shutters that had stood on the corner of a busy intersection of Glades Road and US 1, in Boca Raton, a landmark of sorts, I later found out had been torn down.

My call was transferred from one department to the next before I was finally told they had no prepaid plan for June Wright, only a declaration of her funeral wishes. I already knew what those were so I thanked the woman and hung up.

Pastor Gordon called me the next day. He was clearly on a mission to make sure June would not linger in death as she was in the remainder of her life.

"I'll send you a list of some funeral homes with estimated prices for their prepaid plans," he said.

"Do you have any first hand information of any that are better or more ethical?" I asked. The paper printed a horror story at a local funeral home a few weeks ago and it popped into my mind during this conversation.

"I do and I'll highlight a few of them that I prefer to use," he answered.

"Thank you, Pastor Gordon. Are you Scottish?" I asked. "Gordon was my grandmother's maiden name."

"I most certainly am. Full blooded. I should be wearing a kilt instead of a collar," he joked.

"She was too. Thelma Gordon Husen. Can't get too much more Scottish than that," I said.

"You're mother is a lovely woman. We had a very nice conversation today," Pastor Gordon told me.

I declined to correct him. It wasn't worth expending any more energy on explaining our legal relationship, especially to such a kind, Scottish man of God.

When the list of funeral providers arrived from Pastor Gordon in the mail, he had highlighted the ones he liked best as promised. Top of the list was The Neptune Society. I didn't think I needed to shop around much for a prepaid plan since June didn't care enough to do it for herself.

This had become a pattern with June, assuming things were taken care of when in reality they weren't. Like when she insisted Rosemary and Joe and Darlene, her neighbors, had promised help her if she needed it. They were capable friends and my assistance wasn't necessary, according to her.

When push came to shove, they wanted nothing to do with June. As soon as she moved out of the condo, none of her so-called friends ever called or visited her again. June built an imaginary sense of security around herself in order to prove she was an independent woman. The rest of the world took a very different view of her imaginary well-laid plans.

She had a successful career and supported herself quite well until she married my father. Then where he worked, she worked. They were a package deal in all facets of their lives. He took the job on the condition there was also a position for her. At Rogers Peet in New York City, he had the job of president and June became the ladies dress buyer. When Rogers Peet closed, he moved to Lytton's in Chicago and again June took the position of dress buyer.

In the summer during college, after my mother moved to New York too, June would take me on her visits to dress manufacturers on Seventh Avenue. This was an amazing opportunity for a young college coed majoring in Fashion Merchandising. The show room sales people would ooh and ahh over me and offer free samples I wanted so much to take but was never allowed to have. Ethics you know. What I saw during these trips was a strong role model, asserting herself and making quick decisions. She knew what she liked and had a good eye for what would sell and what wouldn't. June knew her customers.

The vibrant and intelligent side of June faded away so slowly after Dad died and June was left all alone, I didn't notice. My frame of reference of the kind of person June was, remained grounded in my early and most impressionable memories. She was forty-six years old before she ever married, a good long time to become accustomed to an independent way of life. Those habits don't miraculously disappear once the I do's are said. I know because I married at thirty one and even after thirty years of marriage, Richard and I still butt heads over who's in charge of the basics as well as all the other comings and goings in our lives.

At work the next day, I snuck outside so I could talk at least semi-privately. The Neptune Society was my first call. Beth answered the phone. She had a pleasant voice but often hesitated to answer my questions. She must have been new on the job and I was the sale that was going to keep her employed until another payday.

"Our basic package includes cremation and a biodegradable urn," she said.

"She wants to be buried at sea. Is that included?" I asked. Dad had been buried at sea and June only wanted to be with him.

"It's an additional $395." Let the up sell begin. "And it includes..."

I tuned out the rest of the pitch. I was ready to fork over the money right then and there without hesitation. I wasn't in the mood to shop around for a better deal somewhere else. I told Beth exactly that.

"Terrific," she squealed, no longer reading from her script. "Let's get started on the paperwork. "What is your mother's name?"

I had to think here for a minute. Do I give her the legal name or June's switcheroo name she's used most of her life? I had to make a quick decision.

"Dorothy June Wright," I said.

The memorized list of vital information came next. Social security number, last permanent address, married or widowed, children, occupation. The questions seemed to go on forever. Until this one.

"What is her father's name?" Beth asked.

June called him Daddy. I don't think that was what Beth was looking for.

"Let me think a minute." I said. Dad called him by his first name, what was it? Harry, Harvey.

"Harold!" I yelled out. "Cockley." I pronounced it with the incorrect long 'o' but spelled it without the 'a'. Beth would be none the wiser.

"Her mother?" she asked.

"Esther. Esther Wolfe." The name Esther came to mind along with Harold's.

The question and hesitant answer period went on for over a half and hour. I finally gave Beth my credit card number. June could now pass from this world without intervention from others. Due to my disinterest in shopping around for a better deal, Beth would also remain employed.

A week later a box arrived in the mail form the Neptune Society. It contained a gorgeous wooden box, with a highly varnished cherry finish. Inside I found a crystal picture frame and a faux leather folder with a button and an elastic closure, and the biodegradable urn. I was most interested in this last item.

The box dimensions were about eight inches long by five inches wide by five inches tall. It was covered in a dark moss green fabric. A cascade of silk autumn colored leaves adorned the top. I removed the lid and looked inside. A plastic bag ready for the ashes. I examined the container more closely, curious about what made it biodegradable. Cardboard. Dressed up. At least June would be doing her part to save the planet.

"Richard," I shouted. "What am I going to put in here?"

I showed him the contents of the funeral box.

"Wow. What a nice box." His eyes flickered as his brain created a thousand different things he could use it for.

"Don't you want to put June's picture in it and save it for posterity?" I asked.

"You want to keep her ashes? Not in my house." he announced.

"That's creepy keeping her ashes. Do people really do it?" I asked jokingly. I kept the dog's ashes after it died, so why wouldn't people keep other people? Obviously they did or the Neptune Society wouldn't figure the cost of this box and all its contents into the price of its prepaid funeral plan.

"Be sure to tell Pastor Gordon the next time he calls, June's taken care of," Richard said. "Maybe he has a use for the box."

"I want to sleep but my brain won't stop talking to itself." - Anonymous

CHAPTER THIRTY-SIX

Thus continued my secondary education into old age. I'm a baby boomer myself, on the young side of the range of children born after the war, but still considered a boomer. Richard is thirteen years older than I am, so getting ready for the end stage of our lives is something we talk about. Like putting in grab bars in the shower, making sure the will is up to date and most important that neither of us want to be kept alive by any artificial means.

For some reason I have experienced old age diseases at a younger age than my peers. I had a hip replaced at sixty because I could barely walk and the constant pain wore me down, and the ophthalmologist keeps telling me about my cataract that is ripe and read to be removed at age sixty two. I don't know if this is because I hang around with older people, or my body just wore down faster than everyone else.

I hesitate to call this a routine but however sporadic and jumbled these interactions were; they had become my new normal.

Safely tucked in bed reading a book, the phone rang around 9:30 pm.

"Mom's okay," a male voice said without saying hello. "Is this Linda?"

"Yes," I answered.

"June has a skin tear. I'm required to call you whenever that happens." He spoke in a thick Jamaican accent.

"What's a skin tear?" I asked.

"It's a cut on her skin. It's been bandaged and she's resting comfortably," he said.

"Thank you," I said and disconnected the call.

I googled skin tear and the graphic pictures of various shades of red and purple were enough to keep me from sleeping most of the night.

It's 10:00 am and my workday is in full swing. I answered my cell phone.

"Mom's okay. Mrs. Wright has an appointment to see the orthopedic doctor on Friday. Are you available to accompany her?" the voice on the other end of the phone asked.

"No. I live more than a hundred miles away." That's more information than I should offer since the only benefit it serves is to increase the up sell. Or give someone the opportunity to check June's fingers for a fancy diamond since her family didn't show up very often.

"Then you need to call this number and they will send someone to take her," she said.

I called the number and the person on the other end seemed to know June and me personally. There's a conspiracy here, I know it.

"The charge for this service is $75, payable in advance."

Ka-ching.

Do you take a credit card?" I asked.

Of course they did.

After I handed my credit card information into the great unknown, a more important question that I should have asked first popped into my mind.

If June is now under hospice care, why does she have to leave the nursing home to see a doctor? I needed to rewind for minute. The office phone rang and I went back to taking trade orders and requests for funds from a client's brokerage account.

The night, dark and stormy, the rolling rumble of thunder punctuated by the sound of a ringing phone.

"Mom's okay," the voice said. "Is this Linda Wright?"

"Yes it is," I replied.

"My name is Margaret and I'm the hospice nurse. I am here at the Forum to do June's assessment and they won't allow me to see your mom, June," she said. "She's sleeping and they don't want me to wake her since she sleeps so little."

Being unable to sleep was my issue these days. No one had informed me that it was also June's.

"It's after ten. I don't think you should wake her either." Once again I was not going to win any friends after that remark. "Why are you there so late?"

"I just received the assignment and I drove by here on the way home, so I thought I'd stop in." she answered. "I'll come back tomorrow but I wanted to let you know that I'd been here."

"That would be perfect. Thank you," I said. That's why she was sent to the doctor the other day. Hospice dragged its feet sending someone to do an assessment and getting June entered in the program. Until officially enrolled, the nursing home kept on following the normal protocol.

I returned to the less than comforting sounds of Mother Nature hoping desperately the gentle rain falling in the night would soon lull me to dreamless sleep.

The very next day a different nurse called. This time it's Saturday and I'm doing the grocery shopping.

"Mom's okay. Is this Linda?" she asked.

"Yes." I'm learning that a more robust answer isn't necessary.

"We need to change June's room. She sleeps very little and yells quite a bit. It's disturbing the other person in the room." She paused waiting for my response.

"That's fine. Is the not sleeping something new or has it always been that way?" I knew about the yelling from when I visited her in the hospital.

"She never sleeps very well. And she's very disruptive to the other patients," she added. "Dr. Mandel has ordered the psychiatrist to visit with her."

"Can you please make a note in the file to have the doctor call me after the psychiatrist comes to see her?" I asked.

I stare blindly at the shelf of blue pasta boxes, unable to find the boxes of pot-sized spaghetti on my list. I struggle to imagine the kind of conversation June will have with a psychiatrist that will allow the doctor to prescribe the appropriate medicine for her. It goes something like this.

Doctor: Good afternoon, Mrs. Wright. What is your main complaint?

June: Linda put me in this awful place and I just want to go home.

Doctor: Is Linda your daughter?

June: No, I don't have any children.

Doctor: I see. You seem agitated. Tell me what you're feeling.

June: Linda took away my cigarettes and I want a cigarette.

Layers of guilt piled up deep within the folds of my imagination. I blinked my eyes, threw two boxes of bow tie pasta in the cart and moved on to the jars of Ragu.

Doctor: What do you like to do, Mrs. Wright? Do you read books or go to bingo?

June: I smoke cigarettes. Linda took away my vodka too.

Doctor: Why do you think she did that to you?

June: Because she didn't want me to have them.

The rows of spaghetti sauce blurred to red. I grabbed a jar, without paying attention to the brand or the flavor and pushed my cart out of this dreaded aisle. I think we're going to go out for dinner tonight. Too much guilt is swirling around like a pot of boiling noodles.

"Be soft. Do not let the world make you hard. Do not let the bitterness steal your sweetness."

CHAPTER THIRTY-SEVEN

I keep a 5-year journal I write in every night before I go to bed, reflecting on the day. Over the past few years, I'd often written about June. Care and concern for her had consumed much of my daily activities.

March 25, 2015

Early this morning, still in bed, I saw a picture in m mind. I was helping June walk across a bridge. A blue bridge like we had seen in on our trip to Jacksonville crossing the river. At 8 am I was in the shower, the phone rings. June is having trouble breathing. They are calling hospice to put her on crisis care. Someone will be there 24/7.

When the phone rang at 10:30 that night, the nurse didn't start the conversation by saying "Mom's okay." June's suffering was finally over.

* * *

Time is a funny thing, created by man to manage order in our lives. It's finite, and once it's gone, it will never return. Yet time is endless, available for the taking to use however we choose. A lifetime of hardships, headaches and beautiful memories, all mixed together and baked in a bitter but delicious pie raced through my mind in the year since June died. Every day I still wonder if she found the one thing she was looking for and I'll never know the answer to that, at least not while I'm alive. I can only hope that she did. All she ever asked for in the end was to know if Paul would be waiting for her. Knowing she found my father again would bring me some comfort.

I have no understanding of death. None of us do. It's one of those experiences that has to be carried out alone, no one else can do it for you. I pray when my time comes, death will be swift and peaceful. Who doesn't wish for that? How do we need to act while on this Earth and what good deeds do we need to do for God to bestow that on us? I watched June linger far too long as she dwindled toward death. In the grand scheme of things maybe it was no time at all. That's God's little secret and the code will never be cracked.

I had hoped June's death would finally bring her the peace that she longed for. It was not to be. Her death in many ways was the beginning of what might be considered the worst of the injustice.

In her suicide note, June requested no funeral and no obituary. Being pretty pragmatic about death myself, I'm not into hosting a fancy funeral with flowers and eulogies. Her few friends had faded away the minute she began to fail. The rest stopped sending Christmas cards so I assumed June would now be reunited with them on the other side.

I called Susan and gave her the task of informing Martha and Steve. Emotionally drained, I had no energy left to speak to anyone else that evening. Richard and I sat in silence on the couch with our arms around each other for a very long time.

Two days after her death, the funeral director from the Neptune Society called me.

"I want to offer my condolences," he said in a soft voice after introducing himself.

Memories of June floated into my mind constantly in the days following her death. Even though we hadn't grocery shopped together since Richard and I moved away, it suddenly became a chore, not a cherished weekly outing as it had once been. June would show me all the buy one get one bargains she purchased along with her half-gallon of chocolate trinity ice cream. I drifted through the pages of her mail order old ladies clothes catalog that now came to my home with tears in my eyes. The smell of cigarette smoke lingered wherever I went. I knew June watched over me.

"Thank you," I said.

"I'd like to ask you some questions, if you have a few minutes," he asked.

"That's fine," I said.

"Does she have any metal in her body?" he asked.

I went through June's list of artificial parts; several dental implants, a hip replacement, dentures.

"Thank you. I know this isn't easy for you at this time," he consoled. "I have to ask another question. Are you her daughter or her stepdaughter?"

Here we go again, I thought.

"Stepdaughter." Although June taught me how to tell a few little white lies on our journey together, I was not a person who could easily tell any other kind of lie. Not knowing where this line of questioning was headed I didn't sense any need to fudge my answer.

"I have to be sure the arrangements for her are what she wished to have. How long have you known her?" he asked.

"Fifty years," I answered without hesitation.

A pause, "Oh." The only word he could muster at that moment.

He explained since I'm not a blood relative, I would not be able to get a death certificate that included the cause of death.

"Usually insurance companies need the cause of death in order to pay out any proceeds. I'll send you the abbreviated version that should be acceptable for everything else."

He asked for my fax number to send me an affidavit to sign and return.

"An affidavit for what?" I asked.

"You'll have to get it notarized that you knew her for as long as you said you did. Then mail it back to me so I can proceed," he answered.

I brought this conversation to a quick close so I could go have a good hearty cry. She's lying in a freezer somewhere waiting because I'm not a blood relative. Should I have lied? Along the line someone used the word "step" otherwise how would he have known? Why in this day and age of blended families of all shapes and sizes should it make a difference? Am I wicked? Did Cinderella have good reason to despise her stepfamily? Or was she trying to do the right thing? I'm punishing June once again because I simply didn't know how to care for her or give her what she wanted or needed.

Should I have washed my hands of June completely and let her blood relatives take over? Many people gave me that advice over the past few years but interestingly enough that was one decision I had no trouble making. June and I were in this life together.

June left carefully handwritten papers of the nephews and niece addresses and phone numbers. When I emptied her apartment, I packed up the things she wished for them to have and sent them each a letter explaining where she was including her new address and phone number. I receive little response only asking where the rest of their stuff was she had promised them over the years.

The phone numbers on June's list were mostly disconnected. I tried Robin, the lone niece first. All I knew about Robin was she had four daughters and had been widowed at a fairly young age. I think she was about 5 years younger than me. When I couldn't get through to her on the phone number I had, I resorted to informing her of June's death via email. My hand trembled as I pressed the send button. Living in a digital age doesn't mean I should deliver this kind of news over the Internet, but I had no other option. I included my cell phone number if she wanted to talk to me.

In fifty years, I'd never met this woman or any of her brothers. June spoke of them periodically, and shared pictures and cards they sent her at Christmastime but that was all I knew of them. I still often wonder why she kept her blood family separate from Dad's. My sisters and brother knew nothing of this portion of June's life. I knew her best and I feel I knew their names and nothing else about them.

Within a few minutes, my cell phone rang showing a number I didn't recognize.

"Hello?" I answered.

"Linda, it's Robin." Her voice, high pitched, quivering. "I'm in shock."

Shock? Her shallow words shook me to the very bottom of my soul.

"When I spoke to her at Christmas I had the feeling she was failing," Robin said.

Christmas? By last Christmas, June, under hospice care, lived in the nursing home. Robin had all my contact information and never asked me how to reach her aunt. The phone at Hawthorne had been disconnected in October. It's not possible she spoke to June at Christmas. She never even bothered to lend a helping hand or a kind word to her elderly relative.

I don't want a medal. Honestly, I'm glad I didn't have to deal with a committee when it came to making decisions. Each day revealed a new wrinkle to iron out. I often asked Richard and Susan for assistance but they both knew the decision was solely mine. I knew her best.

Robin rattled on how her grown daughters cried when they heard the news, and asked when and where would the funeral be.

"June asked that there be no obituary and no funeral," I said.

"Really? I'm surprised."

I can give you the name of the funeral director. He won't require an affidavit from you, the blood relative intent on carrying out your own wishes instead of the person who's died. I bit my tongue in order not to say what I thought. June would not be lying in a cooler if you or your brothers had stepped in and taken care of her. I had to find a way to end this call before I lost my cool completely.

"She'll be buried at sea with my father. That's what she wanted," I said.

"Where?" Robin asked.

"At sea," I repeated.

"Oh."

"Robin, would you be able to call your brothers and tell them the news?" I asked. "I haven't been able to contact them." I knew what the answer to this question would be but I asked anyway on the chance these relatives would step in and ease my burden one last time.

"I don't speak to my brothers. I don't know how to get in touch with them," she answered.

Terrific. June knew they wouldn't be of any help. That's why she never introduced us. I was on my own and still wishing I didn't have to bear this burden alone. On the other hand I feel blessed I didn't have to share it with someone as clueless as this one.

I let a day pass before trying to call the nephews. I had very pleasant conversations with two of them. Peter thanked me for caring for her and told me stories of a time she visited him in Pennsylvania. How she was so funny and loose compared to his mother who he described as conservative and tight lipped. Larry told me similar tales of funny Aunt June and nice Uncle Paul. He gave his thanks to me too for all I did for her.

The third nephew, Jim, lived in Nebraska somewhere. June constantly worried about him. I never knew why but suspected some kind of bipolar disorder or mental illness. She left no phone number for him, so I only communicated with him through email. He called the lawyer and asked for his money before June had even made it to the after life.

"Problems are like washing machines. They twist, they spin and knock us around; but in the end we come out cleaner and brighter than before."

CHAPTER THIRTY-EIGHT

A year or so after June died; Richard and I visited Asheville, North Carolina. I'd never been there but our mission was to see the Biltmore Estate. Being in the furniture business for so many years, Richard had been to the area many times and was absolutely mesmerized by the Vanderbilts and their sprawling and extravagant estate. The real perk of this trip was that we stayed in a hotel in downtown Asheville across the street from Thomas Wolfe's childhood home.

June had always told me she was Thomas Wolfe's cousin. By the time I found the copies of the family books, and I began researching the writings of Thomas Wolfe, June was unable to remember anything more about the family connection. I was left on my own to try and figure it out. The dates of their births didn't match up as cousins, he was born in 1900, she in 1921. Armed with the names of the Wolfe's I found in the books, I went to tour his Old Kentucky Home. I was the only tourist that day so I received a private guided look through the museum for the price of a group tour.

For me, the house told a fascinating story very similar to what I had read in *Look Homeward Angel*, which is largely thought to be auto-biographical. The house had been restored after a fire set by an arsonist in 1998, but it still retained its early twentieth century look and feel.

The guide walked slowly through the many rooms, explaining which the family used and those rented out to the boarders. The tiny kitchen, with barely enough room for one, turned out meals for all the occupants of the home. Handmade patchwork quilts covered the beds, similar to the ones June's mother handmade, lace doilies graced the dressers and night stands. A strange sense of belonging and familiarity washed over me, in a comforting and calming way.

Afterwards I talked with the museum director and asked her to help me fill in June's family tree. I left my information with her to see if she could connect the dots. It took several weeks but June's mother, Esther, was Thomas' cousin, June's grandfather and W. O. were brothers. She belonged to the Wolfe side of the family that stayed in Pennsylvania. The pieces of the family puzzle began to fall into place.

Outside of the house is a cement pair of Thomas' shoes. He was a big man, 6 foot 6 inches tall. Down the street, I slipped my feet into a cement impression of his size eleven shoes and put my arm around the waist of a life size metal sculpture of the author. Richard snapped our picture.

All the while I felt like June and her famous relative could see me, relishing in watching me traipse around the family home. I made it clear when inside the home it was my stepmother who was related, not me, and that fact made not one bit of difference to any of the people I spoke to. For once the step part of our kindred spirits was not important to anyone. Not even to a brilliant author, Thomas Wolfe, or to those who worked to keep his legacy alive at his museum.

* * *

The second time I was certain I didn't love and respect her any less or her of me was a much different experience. Hurricane Irma had just pounded the state of Florida. Everyone I knew was on edge even days after the storm had passed. That's typical when these kinds of weather events occur and I'd been through many of them in the past. June despised hurricanes, raising her level of panic to a fevered pitch for several days prior and after the landfall. I tried not to let the negative energy seep into my well-being.

A friend needed to vent her lingering frustrations and at the time felt the need to criticize another woman she knew for never visiting her mother in a nursing home. The daughter lived only a few miles away from her aging parent.

"She just can't find the time to see her mother and I think that's disgusting," the friend said.

"It can be a hard thing to do. It forces people to face their own mortality and not everyone wants to look into the future," I replied in the woman's defense.

"But they live in the same town. There's no excuse," she said.

"I can understand how she feels. I couldn't bring myself to visit June," I admitted.

"You lived a hundred miles away and she wasn't really your mother," she replied.

I felt the bile rise into my throat and turned my back on the conversation, all words escaped me. No, June wasn't my mother, but yes, she played an integral part in shaping me from a young age. I had a very different relationship with my own mother who also played a large part in turning me into who I am. Both taught me things about life I loved and embraced. Both exposed me to a dark side of themselves I wanted to turn my back on. I came out the other end a better person for all they gave me.

At that moment, the torn and tattered pieces of my heart mended themselves back together. I did all I could to make sure June lived out the last of her time on earth as comfortably and well as possible. Whether I physically went to see her or not, it made no difference to June. She lived in my heart and I lived in hers.

"I wanted a perfect ending. Now I've learned the hard way, that some poems don't rhyme, and some stories don't have a clear beginning, middle and end." ~ Gilda Radner

EPILOGUE

Whenever I was working on writing this memoir, I carried around a large canvass bag stuffed with all the notes and notebooks I used while navigating the path to the end of June's life. The checklist book I gave her years ago when I had a thought somewhere in the deep recesses of my mind, I needed to know what she wanted in the event of her death weighed down the bag.

Out of curiosity, I opened it again looking for something to complete this story. The book has pages to write in where the will is kept, bank accounts, doctors, lawyers, and insurance policies. June wrote in what she could. Over the years, I'm amazed to say, she updated the book evidenced on the page of important people. All but one had been crossed off with a blue pen when they had died. A snapshot of life and death in our later years was pictured on that page.

I ran my finger down the list of special people who had been a part of my life too. The conduit of memories was because of June. Paper clipped to the inside front cover was a small piece of paper. I did not recognize the handwriting. It wasn't June's. Someone she knew must have thought she would find comfort in it. Did it soothe her to know Dad was waiting for her? Did she know I would find solace in it too? Her way of saying thank you when she was no longer able.

I read the saying aloud.

I give you this one thought to keep,
I am with you still,
I do not sleep.
I am a thousand
Winds that blow,
I am the diamond
Glints on snow,
I am the sunlight
On ripened grain,
I am the gentle Autumn rain.
When you awaken in the
Morning hush, I am the swift,
Uplifting rush of quiet birds in
Circled flight.
I am the soft stars

That shine at night.
Do not think of me as gone.
I am with you still in
Each new dawn.
All is well.